Randi Schmid
'91

MESSAGE OF THE SACRAMENTS

Monika K. Hellwig, Editor

1. **The Catholic Sacraments**
   by Joseph Martos
2. **Gift of Community: Baptism and Confirmation**
   by Thomas A. Marsh
3. **Blessed and Broken: The Contemporary Experience of God in the Eucharist**
   by Ralph A. Keifer
4. **Sign of Reconciliation and Conversion: The Sacrament of Penance for Our Times**
   by Monika K. Hellwig
5. **Christian Marriage: A Journey Together**
   by David M. Thomas
6. **Mission and Ministry: History and Theology in the Sacrament of Order**
   by Nathan Mitchell, OSB
7. **Prophetic Anointing: God's Call to the Sick, the Elderly, and the Dying**
   by James L. Empereur, SJ
8. **Redeemed Creation: Sacramentals Today**
   by Laurence F. X. Brett

The Catholic Sacraments

by

Joseph Martos

A Michael Glazier Book
THE LITURGICAL PRESS
Collegeville, Minnesota

A Michael Glazier Book published by The Liturgical Press.

Copyright © 1983 by Joseph Martos. All rights reserved.

Cover design by Lillian Brulc
Typography by Richard Reinsmith

Printed in the United States of America.
ISBN 0-8146-5227-1

| 3 | 4 | 5 | 6 | 7 | 8 | 9 |

*For my mother, my wife, and my children,
And for the three generations of Catholics
whom they represent*

Contents

Editor's Preface 9
Introduction 11
PART ONE: SACRAMENTS TRANSFORMED ... 15
   I. *Psychology and the Sacraments* 17
  II. *Sociology and the Sacraments* 49
 III. *History and the Sacraments* 86
 IV. *Theology and the Sacraments* 109

PART TWO: SACRAMENTS TRANSFORMING ..171
  V. *The Sacraments and Personal Spirituality* 173
 VI. *The Sacraments and Communal Spirituality* ...183
VII. *The Sacraments and Ecclesial Spirituality*......195
VIII. *The Sacraments and Global Spirituality* 209

Conclusion 225

EDITOR'S PREFACE

This volume is one of the series of eight on *The Message of the Sacraments*. These volumes discuss the ritual practices and understanding and the individual sacraments of the Roman Catholic community. Each of the eight authors has set out to cover five aspects of the sacrament (or, in the first and last volumes, of the theme or issue under discussion). These are: first of all, the existential or experiential meaning of the sacrament in the context of secular human experience; what is known of the historical development of the sacrament; a theological exposition of the meaning, function and effect of the sacrament in the context of present official Catholic doctrinal positions; some pastoral reflections; and a projection of possible future developments in the practice and catechesis of the sacrament.

There is evident need of such a series of volumes to combine the established teaching and firm foundation in sacramental theology with the new situation of the post-Vatican II Church. Because the need is universal, this series is the joint effort of an international team of English-speaking authors. We have not invited any participants whose writing would need to be translated. While we hope that our series will be useful particularly to priests, permanent deacons, seminarians, and those professionally involved in sacramental and catechetical ministries, we also address ourselves confidently to the educated Catholic laity and to those outside the Roman Catholic communion who are interested in learning more about its life and thought. We have all tried to write so as to be easily understood by readers with little or no specialized preparation. We have all tried to deal with the tradition imaginatively but within the acceptable bounds of Catholic orthodoxy, in the firm conviction that that is the way in which we can be most helpful to our readers.

The Church seems to be poised today at a critical juncture in its history. Vatican II reopened long-standing questions about collegiality and participation in the life of the Church, including its sacramental actions, its doctrinal formulations and its government. The Council fostered a new critical awareness and raised hopes which the Church as a vast and complicated institution cannot satisfy without much confusion, conflict and delay. This makes ours a particularly trying and often frustrating time for those most seriously interested in the life of the Church and most deeply committed to it. It seems vitally important for constructive and authentically creative community participation in the shaping of the Church's future life, that a fuller understanding of the sacraments be widely disseminated in the Catholic community. We hope that many readers will begin with the volumes in this series and let themselves be guided into further reading with the bibliographies we offer at the ends of the chapters. We hope to communicate to our readers the sober optimism with which we have undertaken the study and thereby to contribute both to renewal and to reconciliation.

Monika K. Hellwig

INTRODUCTION

It is no secret that the Catholic sacraments are changing, and that our understanding of them is being altered by developments inside and outside the Church. By reading the other books in this series, those who grew up with rather clear and fixed ideas about baptism, confirmation, the Eucharist, marriage, holy orders, penance and the anointing of the sick will discover that the Tridentine practice and theology of the sacraments (with which we lived until quite recently) was rather limited, and that the Catholic Church today is growing beyond those limitations. I have argued in my earlier work, *Doors to the Sacred*, that sacramentality, even in the Church, ought not to be restricted to the seven ecclesiastical sacraments, and other authors in the field have proposed that the rules regulating sacramental worship ought to be relaxed even further than they have already been.

Nevertheless, there are some definite advantages to designating seven distinct church rituals as *the* Catholic sacraments, and to treating them as such within the purview of a single book or a single set of books. It has the ecclesiological advantage of identifying these seven as representative of a distinct denomination within Christianity, the Catholic Church. It has the historical advantage of singling out those rituals which have been referred to as sacraments in the past and about which much has been written. And it has the theological advantage of examining a set of practices in Christian worship which, taken together, touch on all the basic aspects of Christian life.

What we say about these sacraments must therefore have some continuity with the past, but even so it must not be restricted to repeating what was said in the past. We must even sometimes reevaluate past Catholic teachings when we have reason to suspect that the theologians who formulated those teachings were mistaken about scientific and historical facts or limited in their intellectual horizons. At the same time, however, we must be appreciative of the good in earlier practices and theological formulations, tolerant of those in earlier periods and other cultures which differ from our own, and sensitive to those in the Church today whose sacramental world was shaped before the Second Vatican Council.

The main challenge of writing an introductory volume such as this one, however, is to say something about all the sacraments without simply repeating what the other authors in the series will be saying about each of them. I was able through the generosity of our publisher, Michael Glazier, to read the manuscripts of most of the other volumes before they went to press, and trusting that the reader will supplement what is said in these pages with the details to be found in the other books, I have attempted to sketch a rather general picture of the Catholic Church's sacramental system. Our editor for the series, Monika Hellwig, asked that each volume say something about the experience, history and theology of the sacraments, and about their pastoral and practical implications. I have tried to respond to her invitation by examining the sacraments from the viewpoints of psychology, sociology, history and theology in Part One, and then by discussing the sacraments in the contexts of the individual, the local community, the institutional Church and the world at large in Part Two.

The reader will notice that there is a difference in length

and style between the chapters in Part One and those in Part Two. This is deliberate. The first four chapters are reportive and explanatory, for they present what can be said about the sacraments from various intellectual perspectives, and so they are longer and they indicate in footnotes where further information about the variety of topics may be found. The second four chapters are reflective and exploratory, for they suggest theological implications of the sacraments in various dimensions of Christian life, and so they are shorter and they proclaim the message of the sacraments simply and without footnotes.

PART ONE: SACRAMENTS TRANSFORMED

In his preface to Raymond Vaillancourt's *Toward a Renewal of Sacramental Theology,* Clement Farly wrote:

> The need for a new way of talking about the sacraments is felt on all sides. It is no longer enough to repeat the language of a former age; instead it has become indispensable to invent once again a language that is intelligible to our contemporaries, a language that cannot be accused of reflecting a magical mentality but will nonetheless express the dynamism of the sacraments in all its fullness, without any watering down. This is a task that can no longer be avoided.

Until recently, we Catholics did not fully appreciate how much the language of our theology had been shaped by ancient philosophy and medieval metaphysics. Those were the sciences of ages past, and intellectually-minded Christians used them to understand every aspect of the Christian life, including the sacraments. In our own century, however, the sciences of psychology, sociology and history have opened up further possibilities for understanding ourselves, and new philosophies have shed additional light on many dimensions of reality both human and divine.

If we are to speak coherently about the sacraments to our

present age (and indeed to ourselves), we must use the insights that the modern sciences give us into the forces that have transformed and continue to influence our sacramental experience. And we must slowly transform the way we speak about the sacraments, not forgetting the language of traditional theology, but getting behind that language and keeping in touch with the realities that it talked about.

CHAPTER I: PSYCHOLOGY AND THE SACRAMENTS

Sacraments are not for the unconscious, the asleep or the dead. They are for the awake and aware, the living and growing. Sacraments are signs, and they function as symbols: they resonate in the thoughts and feelings of those who perceive them. Sacraments are actions, and they function as rituals: they repeat gestures and words that are meaningful to those who perceive them. Sacraments are not merely symbolic rituals, but they are at least that, and they must be understood as such.

1. Psychological Dimensions of the Sacraments

In the early 1960s two books appeared in English which had a dramatic impact on Catholic sacramental theology: Edward Schillebeeckx's *Christ, the Sacrament of the Encounter with God*, and Bernard Cooke's *Christian Sacraments and Christian Personality*. They reminded us of the broadly psychological dimensions of our sacramental celebrations which traditional theology had tended to neglect or obscure. Schillebeeckx pointed out that in each sacrament we come in contact with the saving presence and power of Christ, and that on our part this should be an existentially personal encounter. Cooke showed how in responding to the grace that is offered in each of the sacraments our personality becomes more Christ-like.[1] After that, Catholic authors paid further attention to the experiential dimensions of the sacraments, most notably Aidan Kavanagh and Joseph Powers. In 1967 Kavanagh observed, "Ritual is the hinge on which personal interiorization of religious tradition swings, the experiential source from which a sense of religious identity, dedication, renewed freedom and effectiveness proceeds."[2] And in 1973 in *Spirit and Sacrament* Powers explored the experiences that are pointed to through the linguistic symbols, "God," "Spirit," "Christ" and "Church," and further in the context of the sacraments, "grace," "salvation," "rebirth" and "forgiveness."[3] In the years since, it has become increasingly taken for granted that participating in and reflecting on the sacraments should have psychological ramifications.

Of course, this understanding has never been entirely absent from Catholic theology. St. Paul was undoubtedly reflecting on his own religious experience when he formulated many of his teachings,[4] and similarly the Fathers of the Church and the early scholastics often used symbolic language to express what they felt was otherwise ineffable. The same has been true of the great Christian mystics, St. Teresa of Avila, St. John of the Cross, and others. But in the Middle Ages Catholic theology developed a technical language that was objective and metaphysical, with the result that the subjective and experiential dimensions of doctrine

---

[1] Edward Schillebeeckx, *Christ the Sacrament of the Encounter with God* (New York: Sheed and Ward, 1963); Bernard Cooke, *Christian Sacraments and Christian Personality* (New York: Holt, Rinehart and Winston, 1965).

[2] Aidan Kavanagh, O.S.B., "How Rite Develops: Some Laws Intrinsic to Liturgical Evolution," *Worship* 41 (1967) p. 342. See also Kavanagh's many articles on liturgy and sacraments in *Worship* and other journals during this period.

[3] Joseph Powers, S.J., *Spirit and Sacrament* (New York: Seabury Press, 1973). See also his *Eucharistic Theology* (New York: Herder and Herder, 1967).

[4] This shows through most clearly in such passages as Rom. 5-8, I Cor. 2-4, 7-14, II Cor. 4-6, 10-12, and Gal. 2-4.

were often relegated to the realms of personal piety. To some extent the liturgical renewal, which began with the Benedictines during the last century and is continuing in our own, reintroduced Catholics to the psychological dimension of liturgical spirituality. This dimension was recognized in such books as *The Inner Life of Worship* and in many of the writings of Thomas Merton.[5] As summarized in the words of the Maritains, Jacques and Raissa,

> The worship rendered to God by the Church is necessarily an exterior worship, but it is a worship in spirit and in truth, in which what matters above all is the interior movement of souls and the divine grace operating in them.[6]

Even before the Second Vatican Council, reputable theologians such as Henri de Lubac, Piet Fransen and Karl Rahner acknowledged that the supernatural reality of grace was something that entered the realm of human consciousness, and after the council the experience of grace got further attention from Catholic authors.[7] Moreover, religious conversion is an area of religious experience in which the psychological aspects have long been recognized (think, for example, of St. Augustine's *Confessions*). And finally, some of the sacraments have normally been expected to have psychological implications for those who participated

---

[5]Charles M. Magsam, M.M., *The Inner Life of Worship* (St. Meinrad, Indiana: Grail Publications, 1958). See, for example, Thomas Merton's *The Living Bread* (New York: Farrar, Straus and Cudahy, 1956).

[6]Jacques and Raissa Maritain, *Liturgy and Contemplation* (New York: P.J. Kenedy and Sons, 1960) p. 14f.

[7]This is not to suggest, of course, that everything referred to in the traditional theology of grace is available to our experience. On this subject, see Piet Fransen, S.J., "Towards a Psychology of Divine Grace" written in 1954 and collected in *Intelligent Theology*, Vol. III (Chicago: Franciscan Herald Press, 1969) pp. 7-45; Karl Rahner, S.J., "Concerning the Relationship Between Nature and Grace," *Theological Investigations*, Vol. I (Baltimore: Helicon Press, 1961) esp. pp. 298, 300; also his "Reflections on the Experience of Grace," *Theological Investigations*, Vol. III (Baltimore: Helicon Press, 1967) pp. 86-90; William W. Meissner, S.J., *Foundations for a Psychology of Grace* (Glen Rock, New Jersey: Paulist Press, 1966).

in them: the Eucharist, as the sacrament of Christ's presence and God's love, and Penance, as the sacrament of human contrition and divine compassion. (It is perhaps noteworthy that of the seven, these two are ordinarily the only two frequently repeatable sacraments.)

2. The Sacred Dimension

Those engaged in the scientific study of religion today acknowledge that the sacred is a genuine dimension of human consciousness. Although not all people can point to times in their lives when they have felt what they might call the presence of God or the power of grace, there are many who can. In tribal and ancient societies psychological encounters with the sacred were considered normal and what was experienced in those moments was regarded as real. The same was true to a greater or lesser extent in traditional Christian society. In today's secular society there is a tendency to dismiss such experiences as "merely psychological," but people who do so apparently do not recognize that *all* human experiences (including the experience of colors, sounds, smells, tastes and touches) are at root psychological.[8] Thus in the psychology of religion, the sociology of religion, and the history of religion the experience of the sacred, the divine or the transcendent is regarded as an authentically human experience. "It is as if there were in human consciousness a sense of reality, a feeling of objective presence, a perception of what may be called 'something there'."[9]

---

[8] On this point, the history of modern philosophy from Descartes and Locke onward bears adequate testimony. For a brief and clear exposition of this matter, see Garrett Barden and Philip McShane, *Towards Self Meaning* (New York: Herder and Herder, 1974) pp. 42-47. On the reason why the complete subjectivity of our experience does not imply the complete subjectivity of human knowledge, see Bernard Lonergan, S.J., *Insight: A Study of Human Understanding* (New York: Philosophical Library, 1957).

[9] William James, *The Varieties of Religious Experience* (New York: Random House Modern Library edition, 1932) p. 58 (italics deleted).

That "something there" was extensively described in 1917 by Rudolf Otto in his now classic study, *The Idea of the Holy*.[10] In its most intensive moments the object of that experience appears to be "wholly other," a *mysterium tremendum et fascinans*, a mystery which is at the same time both frightening and fascinating, a "numinous reality" charged with power and radiating energy, to which we respond with feelings of reverence and awe. In less intensive moments it is experienced as no less real but still indescribable, familiar yet strange, sublime and deserving of respect. Experiences of this sort are so characteristic of religious life that religion itself has sometimes been defined in relation to them.[11]

When we encounter the holy in our own lives (and Christians tend to designate these moments as experiences of God or experiences of grace) we enter, as it were, another dimension of reality. It is called in contemporary religious studies the world or realm of the sacred, in contrast to the ordinary, profane, everyday world that we normally inhabit.[12] It is a world in which we have an altered sense of space and time: the space which we inhabit is somehow sanctified, and the time or period in which it occurs is likewise made holy. At some times, it is not unlike the experience of being in love, and of being in the presence of one's beloved. At other times, it is more like the experience of what Protestants call "conviction," an awareness of their sinfulness and guilt in the presence of the One who is all pure and all good. There is a

---

[10] Rudolf Otto, *The Idea of the Holy* (New York: Oxford University Press edition, 1950). For a more contemporary account of this and other religious experiences, see William F. Kraft, *The Search for the Holy* (Philadelphia: Westminster Press, 1971).

[11] For example, "'Religion,' it might be said, is the term that designates the attitude peculiar to a consciousness which has been altered by the experience of the numinosum." G. Stephens Spinks, *Psychology and Religion* (Boston: Beacon Press, 1967) p. 6.

[12] Note that "world" here is understood psychologically, (or more accurately, phenomenologically) in the sense that each of us may be said to live at the center of our own world, or that the world of the scientist is different from the world of the artist.

wide variety of such religious experiences.[13] And yet they all seem to take place in what Mircea Eliade calls sacred space and sacred time.[14]

Very often the occasions for these religious experiences (Eliade calls them "hierophanies" or manifestations of the sacred) are particular objects and gestures, places and occasions which have come to be regarded as special and sacred in themselves.[15] For primitive peoples these are very often things associated with nature, such as certain plants and stones, particular mountains and rivers, the winter solstice and spring time. For Catholics and other Christians they tend rather to be such things as relics and statues, churches and shrines, scriptures and hymns, liturgies and sacraments, Christmas and Easter time. In the technical language of religious studies, objects and rites, places and occasions of this sort are perceived by believers as possessing "mana," a numinous power or supernatural aura which penetrates them and radiates from them.[16] Persons too can be imbued with mana, but following the suggestion of the pioneering sociologist Max Weber, such personal mana is usually referred to in religious studies as "charisma." In the history of religions Moses and Jesus, Buddha and Mohammed, and other great religious leaders have all been seen by their

---

[13] See Gordon Allport, *The Individual and His Religion* (New York: Macmillan, 1960) p. 29; also James, pp. 42-49.

[14] See Mircea Eliade, *The Sacred and the Profane* (New York: Harcourt, Brace and World, 1959) pp. 20-65, 68-95. For a more scholarly treatment, see his *Patterns in Comparative Religion* (New York: Sheed and Ward, 1958) pp. 367-408. For a discussion of these phenomena more related to contemporary religious experience, see John E. Smith, *Experience and God* (New York: Oxford University Press, 1968) pp 57-62.

[15] See Eliade, *Patterns*, pp. 2-4, 8-13, 23-30. See also Bernard Lonergan, *Method in Theology* (New York: Herder and Herder, 1972) p. 108f.

[16] *Mana* is originally a Melanesian word, but it has been adopted by anthropologists and others to refer to what is called *wakan, orenda, maga* (an ancient Persian word with the same root as our "magic") and so on in various tribal cultures. The reality to which these words point seems to be a fairly universal phenomenon in all religions both primitive and modern. For a good summary treatment of mana, see Barbara Hargrove, *The Sociology of Religion* (Arlington Heights, Illinois: AHM Publishing Corporation, 1979) pp. 16-18.

followers as having sacred powers or qualities. In the history of Judaism and Christianity, the kings and prophets of Israel, the martyrs and saints of the church, as well as individuals such as Augustine and Chrysostom, Luther and Calvin, Pope John XXIII and Martin Luther King have been perceived as charismatic persons. Finally, persons can come to be regarded as having charismata worthy of respect in virtue of their office or function in a religious society, for example, priests and bishops, nuns and religious superiors, evangelists and healers.[17]

In traditional Christianity, the religious experience which is pointed to in contemporary religious studies by such words as "hierophany," "mana" and "charisma" is the experience of mystery. Intellectually, mystery can be conceived of as something which is only partially understood and never completely understandable; on the level of experience, however, mystery is perceived to be present when we have a sense of the sacred, the numinous, the more than natural.[18] In this sense the experience of the disciples on Pentecost, of St. Paul on the road to Damascus, of St. Peter when he had his dream, and of countless other saints and mystics can all be classified as hierophanies. But so too can the even more frequent experiences in which ordinary Christians sense the presence of God or the power of grace. "In this perspective," says Jean Mouroux, "religious experience can be defined as the act — or group of acts — through which man becomes aware of himself in relation to God." Thus, "one may say that God is not given in experience but grasped in it."[19] Similarly, people who saw the power of God in Jesus' miracles, or who sensed the dyna-

---

[17]Note that in sociology "charisma" is a religiously neutral term, so that even great secular leaders can be referred to as charismatic individuals: persons like Elizabeth I, Napoleon, Churchhill, even Hitler. See Thomas F. O'Dea, *The Sociology of Religion* (Englewood Cliffs, New Jersey: Prentice Hall, 1966) pp. 22-24; also Max Weber, *On Charisma and Institution Building* (Chicago: University of Chicago Press, 1968).

[18]On this point, see Jean Mouroux, *The Christian Experience* (New York: Sheed and Ward, 1954) pp. 17-20.

[19]Mouroux, p. 15, p. 21.

mism of the Holy Spirit in the apostles' laying on of hands, or who felt a supernatural regeneration through the ritual of adult baptism, or who were aware of a divine presence in the Eucharistic host — in the language of secular religious studies they can be said to have experienced mana, while in the language of Christianity they can be said to have experienced mystery, or some aspect of the divine mystery. In fact, for most Christians the encounter with mystery is "a mediated experience. The presence and grasp of God which it involves are both realized through the mediation of a sign, or series of signs."[20] Finally, for Christians the primary person imbued with charisma and radiating divine power is the figure of Jesus. Those who walked with him in Palestine, who bore testimony to his resurrection, and who acknowledged him as the Christ sensed in his person the spirit of God. For them and for all Christians afterward, *the* mystery of Christianity is the mystery of Christ, believed certainly, but primarily experienced as the mystery of God himself.

In contemporary Christianity, however, both in liberal Protestantism and increasingly in Catholicism, there seems to be a loss of the sense of mystery, an absence of the traditional types of religious experience such as those just described. Although there are notable exceptions to this trend, Christians in general seem to have a harder time seeing God at work in their everyday lives than, say, their parents and grandparents did. Catholics in particular seem to find it more difficult to sense the mysterious power of the sacraments or even to experience the presence of Christ in the Eucharist.[21] And there are those, both Protestant and Catholic, who find it more comfortable to relate to Jesus as a good man, perhaps even as a prophet or a great man, than to encounter him as God's incarnate Word.

There appear to be a number of reasons for this decline in

---

[20]Mouroux, p. 21.

[21]On some of the reasons for this development in relation to the sacrament of penance, see Monika Hellwig's Introduction to her book in this series, *Sign of Reconciliation and Conversion* (Wilmington, Delaware: Michael Glazier, 1982).

the experience of the sacred, the psychological sense of mystery. One which is often pointed to is the gradual secularization of society. As the secrets of nature become known to science, as the world becomes more filled with the products of technology, as people's affairs become less regulated by religious institutions and more regulated by secular institutions, God seems to become less and less relevant to their daily lives. Along this line one can also point to contemporary religious studies, to the "demythologizing" of the scriptures which seems to rob them of their literal truth, to the "sociologizing" of the Church which makes it look like just one more institution among many, and even the "psychologizing" of religious experience which seems to make it just another human, but all too human, experience. Another factor seems to be that traditional religious language and symbols (like the doctrine of original sin, the symbol of the Sacred Heart, or even the pastoral imagery of the New Testament parables) no longer connect with people's experience of themselves and their world. Along with this, traditional Christian spirituality often seemed to demand self-abasement and slavish dependence on God and the clergy, but these are attitudes which today appear strange if not perverse to people seeking self-fulfillment and personal and social liberation.[22] One can point to other factors as well, including (for Catholics especially) a loss of a sense of personal community, a disenchantment with Church authority, a weakening of institutional identity in the wake of the changes wrought by Vatican II, and even the rejection of the belief that the sacraments are magically effective.[23]

---

[22]See Harvey Cox, *The Secular City* (New York: Macmillan, 1965); Gregory Baum, "Religious Experience and Doctrinal Statements" in George Devine, ed., *New Directions in Religious Experience* (New York: Alba House, 1971) esp. pp. 5 and 9f.

[23]On this point, I suspect on anthropological grounds that the rejection may be premature. Not long ago it was abhorrent to think that certain biblical stories might be myths; today that view is commonly accepted, due in part to a greater appreciation and understanding of myth as a valid form of human communication. Similarly, I believe that a parallel rethinking and rehabilitation of the nature

Anthropologist Mary Douglas, however, has argued that there is another key factor at work in the diminishing experience of the sacred. In her book *Natural Symbols* she demonstrates that socially static and hierarchically organized societies are more prone to express their religious ideas in ritual and to respond to the symbolism of such ritual. The reasons for this are apparently psychological in as much as in static, stratified societies people tend to accept things "the way they are" in both the natural and supernatural orders. These rituals are plausible, and people can "see through" the symbols to the realities that they symbolize without much difficulty. Moreover, these rituals are acknowledged to be efficacious, for people in such societies easily believe in the mysterious effects that the rites are supposed to have, such as appeasing the gods through sacrifice or having a demon dispelled through exorcism.[24] As Catholic society goes through its present period of turmoil, therefore, the traditional sacraments (which are symbolic rituals) become less capable of conveying a common understanding of God, or even of mediating a common experience of the sacred. In other words, fixed and standardized religious rituals work well only in stable and stratified societies. And so to the extent that the culture of European and American Catholicism is changing and destratifying (as it seems to be), to that extent standard rituals such as the sacraments are less effective symbols than they used to be. Put succinctly, "when the social group grips its members in tight communal bonds, religion is ritualistic; when this grip is relaxed, ritualism declines."[25]

This does not mean, however, that experiences of the

and function of magic in earlier cultures may shed great light on medieval religion and sacramental theology.

[24] See Mary Douglas, *Natural Symbols* (New York: Random House Vintage Books edition, 1973) esp. chs. 1-4.

[25] Douglas, p. 32. Note that Douglas' analysis also suggests why elaborate religious ritual is still effective in Eastern Europe and Russia, and in highly structured groups such as monastic orders. She also gives more than a hint that highly ritualistic religion and belief in its magical efficacy is natural and normal in rigidly stratified societies.

sacred or encounters with mystery are entirely absent from people's lives today. It implies only that when such experiences occur, they often do not occur in traditional religious contexts like standardized church rituals. For religious people, such experiences tend to occur more frequently in periods of private prayer, in the individual reading of the scriptures, or in the context of small religious groups. For non-religious people they occur in analogous moments of meditation, in reading literature and poetry, in viewing films and plays, and in interpersonal encounters. Psychologist Abraham Maslow refers to such moments as "peak experiences."

> In moments of such experience, one is gathered up into a vision of the universe as a coherent unity to which one feels intimately related. One is delivered from egoistic concerns into a clearer perception of others as well as one's own uniqueness.... This experience is self-validating; it needs no external justification. Values are sacred; emotions of awe and surrender predominate; dichotomies are transcended; fear and confusion are left behind. One feels more receptive in one's cognition, more able to love and to respond to others and to life as a whole.[26]

Maslow also admits the occurrence of "plateau experiences," which are heightened if not peak moments of existential awareness. These are less rare and they are more liable to be repeated in situations such as religious and civil and even personal ritual. When they happen, and especially when they repeat themselves, such heightened moments of awareness tend to be touched off by the occurrence of a situation or the appearance of a signal which seems to function as a symbol for them. Indeed, most sacramental experiences appear to fit the description of plateau experiences rather

---

[26] Ann and Barry Ulanov, *Religion and the Unconscious* (Philadelphia: Westminster Press, 1975) p. 52f. See also Abraham H. Maslow, *Religions, Values and Peak Experiences* (New York: Viking Press, 1970) and Charles R. Meyer, *The Touch of God* (New York: Alba House, 1972).

than peak experiences, for they gather together in a moment of heightened awareness a re-realization of values, beliefs and feelings which have already been experienced and affirmed as sacred.

3. The Symbolic Dimension

In contemporary philosophy, it was largely through the work of Ernst Cassirer and Susanne Langer that we began to understand the value and importance of symbols.[27] Until recently Catholics thought of their sacraments primarily as signs, perhaps because medieval theology did not work out the ramifications of the difference between signs and symbols. St. Augustine and St. Thomas Aquinas both defined sacrament as "a sign of something sacred," and similarly the Baltimore Catechism said, "A sacrament is an outward sign instituted by Christ to give grace."[28] But Catholic theology also understood that the sacraments were a special kind of sign: they were "effective signs." Today we realize that part of their effectiveness, at least, is due to their being symbols.

There are a number of ways of differentiating signs from symbols.[29] For our purposes, perhaps the best way is to do it psychologically, that is, in terms of how they affect us and how we respond to them. We can say that signs tend to affect us simply and we tend to respond to them simply, but symbols tend to affect us complexly and we tend to respond to them complexly. Perhaps in terms of the meaning that

---

[27] See Ernst Cassirer, *The Philosophy of Symbolic Forms* (New Haven: Yale University Press, 3 vols., 1953, 1955, 1957) esp. vol. II, *Mythical Thought*; also Susanne Langer, *Philosophy in a New Key* (Cambridge, Massachusetts: Harvard University Press, 3rd ed., 1957).

[28] St. Augustine, *Letters*, no. 138, 1; St. Thomas Aquinas, *Summa Theologica*, III, q. 60, a. 2; *A Catechism of Christian Doctrine* (Paterson, New Jersey: St. Anthony Guild Press, 1941 edition) q. 304.

[29] See, for example, Langer, pp. 57-59; Thomas Fawcett, *The Symbolic Language of Religion* (Minneapolis: Augsburg Publishing House, 1971) chs. 1 and 2; George S. Worgul, Jr., *From Magic to Metaphor* (New York: Paulist Press, 1980) ch. 3.

they have for us, we can say that signs come across to us as having a basic denotation (or meaning) and not much connotation (or associated meaning), whereas symbols may even have many denotations and they are rich in connotations.[30] Some illustrations may make this clearer. Ordinarily, words are simply signs for us. They are signs of what the words mean, or of what they stand for. Like the words in this sentence that you are reading: they have meaning for you, and the meaning registers. Simple input, simple response. Or the signs on the doors that say ENTRANCE and EXIT; you know what they mean, and you use the right door. Or the road signs in Europe, which do not use words but indicate "Stop" and "No parking" and so on. These are all conventional, man-made, artificial signs. But there are also natural signs. Smoke is a sign of fire. Laughter in a room means that people are having a good time. Trees turning green is a sign of spring.

Things that usually function as signs, however, can sometimes function as symbols. Words like "God," "freedom," "sex" and so on can evoke subtle emotions even by themselves, and when used in the context of a religious sermon or a political speech they can resonate deep in our feelings. We react to sentences like "I love you" and "You're a pig" not because of what they blandly denote but because of what they powerfully connote to us. Our country's flag and national anthem are not just cloth and music, but they remind us in our depths of memories and beliefs, ideals and values, hopes and fears that we share in common with so many others. Again, words, emblems, music and the like are conventional symbols, but there are also natural symbols. The greening of springtime can symbolize for us the end of winter confinement, invigorating freshness, the promise of

---

[30] I realize that the English language does not always use the words "sign" and "symbol" according to these psychological criteria. For example, what we ordinarily call mathematical symbols would here be classified as signs, and what are ordinarily called signs of affection would here be called symbols. But anyone who treats the subject of signs and symbols faces this same difficulty. I can only hope my meaning is clear despite the vagaries of everyday language.

summer's warmth, and hope for new beginnings. And it is hard to be kissed (especially unexpectedly) without feeling and thinking of a number of things simultaneously.

Interestingly, almost anything can be viewed as a sign or symbol of something else, if it is taken that way. Books can be just books, or they can be taken as a sign of learning. Fire can be just fire, or it can be taken as a symbol of warmth and life, or conversely, of destruction and death. Because of this, signs and symbols are said to "point to" what they signify; they refer to something else besides themselves. But whereas things taken as signs usually have a single or simple referent (like the label on a box to what is inside it), things taken as symbols have a multiple or complex referent (they can mean many things simultaneously). Because signs or symbols do not stand simply for themselves, they sometimes have to be interpreted or deciphered or translated for those who do not know what they mean or refer to.

In the current literature on religious symbolism, the ability of symbols to have multiple or complex meanings is designated by a variety of terms: multivalence, multivocality, coalescence of meaning, richness of expression, condensation, polysemy, and surplus of meaning.[31] All these terms, however, refer to the same basic fact, namely that when some object or image or natural phenomenon is apprehended symbolically, it conveys many things simultaneously. As Mircea Eliade insists, it is a drastic mistake to reduce a symbolic image to just one of its meanings:

> It is therefore the image as such, the whole bundle of meanings that is *true*, not any *one* of its meanings, nor one alone of its many frames of reference. To translate an image into a concrete terminology by restricting it to any one of its frames of reference is to do worse than mutilate it — it is to annihilate, to annul it as an instrument of cognition.[32]

---

[31] See Victor W. Turner, *Forest of Symbols* (Ithaca, New York: Cornell University Press, 1967) pp. 50-52; Fawcett, p. 28f; Langer, pp. 94-97.

[32] Mircea Eliade, *Images and Symbols* (New York: Sheed and Ward, 1961) p. 15. See also his *Patterns*, ch. 13.

One of the ways that symbols get their ability to communicate many things to us at the same time is through the psychological association of overt or surface meanings with covert or subliminal meanings and feelings. At least some of the meanings of any symbol are hidden or depth meanings when the symbol is doing its work. Modern day advertisers know this much about the psychology of symbolism very well, which is why they often associate the products they are selling (the overt message) with symbols of sex, power, wealth, motherhood, patriotism, or anything else which will make us feel positively about them (the covert message). Psychologically sophisticated advertising thus carries a double message, although in this case the connection between the overt and covert messages is often contrived and usually manipulative in intent.[33] In the ordinary use of symbols, the association between the levels of meaning is more spontaneous and natural, and the intent is communicative: to say in symbol what cannot be said otherwise.

Anthropologist Victor Turner has documented how these two levels of meaning relate to one another in the religious rituals of tribal and other cultures.[34] Borrowing Turner's analytical ideas (but not his technical terminology),[35] we can say that when a symbol resonates in our minds and hearts, it is often because meanings and feelings at the depth level of the symbol get psychologically associated with meanings and images at the surface level of the symbol. Thus at the surface level, for example, a picture of Our Lady of Lourdes refers to Mary, the mother of Jesus, and her appearance to

---

[33] The classic work on this subject is Vance Packard, *The Hidden Persuaders* (New York: David McKay, 1957).

[34] For a good summary of Turner's ideas, as well as references to his other works, see Appendix A of Victor and Edith Turner, *Image and Pilgrimage in Christian Culture* (New York: Columbia University Press, 1978) pp. 243-255. Turner's work has already begun to be applied by Catholic scholars to the sacraments. See, for example, Michael G. Lawler, "Christian Rituals: An Essay in Sacramental Symbolisms," *Horizons* 7(1980) pp. 7-35; also Worgul, pp. 98-104.

[35] His terminology is quite precise, though not very descriptive. Turner analyzes symbols by grouping them around what he terms the orectic (or sensory) pole and the ideological (or normative) pole. I prefer to call them the depth and surface levels of meaning, or the generic and specific meanings, of a symbol.

St. Bernadette. But at the depth level (for those who are open to it) the symbol evokes meanings and feelings associated with motherhood, virginity, divinity and compassion (since she was the virgin mother of God who deigned to appear to a peasant). Or to take another example, oil had a set of culturally accepted meanings in the Middle East around the time of Christ: oil was used as a salve and medicine, and so it meant health and healing; it was used to moisten dry skin and hair, and so it meant leisure and luxury; it was used to anoint priests and kings, and so it meant divine presence and power. And so when anointing became part of the Christian initiation ritual (and it was in part because of this rich complex of cultural meanings that it came to be used in the ritual), although it now also had Christian meanings attached to it, the use of oil brought with it a whole host of generic meanings which reinforced those specifically Christian meanings and aroused ideas and ideals, feelings and desires that had been traditionally associated with oil.[36]

The fact that Marian devotion is on the wane in contemporary Catholicism, however, and the fact that the use of oil in our sacraments no longer calls forth the depth meanings that it had in the ancient world illustrate that neither the intellectual nor the psychological effectiveness of symbols is automatic. Just as personal symbols may not mean to others what they mean to us, so ecclesial symbols of the Christian experience of the sacred may not mean to one generation or culture what it means to others. Nor is the situation unique to Catholicism. Protestant theologian Paul Tillich has observed about symbols, "They grow when the situation is ripe for them, and they die when the situation changes."[37] Normally when a symbol stops being significant to people, they stop using it. In today's world many in religious orders

---

[36] Another book in this series, *Blessed and Broken* by Ralph Keifer (Wilmington, Delaware: Michael Glazier, 1982) applies this analysis to the Paschal Vigil in ch. 6. Keifer refers to the orectic meanings as the human element or the primal layer in the symbolic experience.

[37] Paul Tillich, *Dynamics of Faith* (New York: Harper and Row, 1958) p. 43.

have stopped wearing their traditional habit because it no longer expresses what they want to say about themselves, and people are not buying traditional statues and pictures because such art no longer speaks to them. This fact is more adequately demonstrated in the history of religious symbolism, and even in the way that the symbols and rituals of a religion other than our own can seem odd and foreign to us. "Symbols are effective only so long as they are relevant to life," and so, "when a symbol loses its meaning it may continue as a historical sign but as a symbol it is dead."[38]

At the same time, however, there are some fundamental *types* of religious symbols that seem to never die. Mircea Eliade has abundantly demonstrated that although individual symbols may come and go, there are some general symbolic types which keep recurring in the history of religion: sky symbolisms of transcendence and infinity, sun and fire symbolisms of light and life, moon and seasonal symbolisms of cyclical renewal, rock and stone symbolisms of stability and endurance, tree and plant symbolisms of life and growth, water symbolisms of potentiality and ambiguity.[39] To these fundamental nature symbols we must add physical human realities such as masculinity and femininity, genital sexuality, blood and menstrual flow, plus common human gestures such as laughter and tears, embracing and distancing, food sharing and abstinence, postures of authority and submission, and so forth.[40] Eliade calls these general and basic types of symbols "archetypes" or fundamental symbolic images, as does psychologist Carl Jung, who found such recurring symbolism not only in the dreams of his patients but also in many of the world's religions:

> The fact is that certain ideas exist almost everywhere and at all times and they spontaneously create themselves

---

[38]Spinks, p. 98 (italics deleted).

[39]For many of these, see his *Patterns*, cited above.

[40]For many of these, see Victor Turner, *Dramas, Fields and Metaphors: Symbolic Action in Human Society* (Ithaca, New York: Cornell University Press, 1974).

quite apart from migration and tradition. They are not made by the individual but rather they happen — they even force themselves on the individual's consciousness.[41]

This sort of archetypal symbolism is found not only in religious objects, images and gestures; it is also found in religious stories or myths. Although the words "myth" and "mythic" once had exclusively pejorative connotations (and the words are still used this way in ordinary speech), contemporary religious studies understand myth to be a fundamental form of symbolic narrative, an expression of symbols in story form. In this sense of the term, creation accounts in the Old Testament and the infancy narratives in the New Testament, for example, are today accepted as mythic in character, for they attempt to say in the concrete imagery of story what their authors undestood about the human situation and about the person of Jesus.[42] Moreover, just as one finds repeated patterns of archetypal symbols in the world's religions, so also one finds repeated archetypal patterns and images in religious myths. There are stories about the creation of the world and about the origins of everything that is important to human beings; there are stories about gods and goddesses, heroes and heroines, and how they interact with one another; there are stories which show how to do things (like hunting and farming), how to make things (such as homes and boats), and how to behave in various situations (as in times of danger or in times of celebration).[43]

---

[41] Karl Jung, *Psychology and Religion* (New Haven, Connecticut: Yale University Press, 1932) p. 4.

[42] On myth in general, see Ernst Cassirer, *An Essay on Man* (New Haven, Connecticut: Yale University Press, 1944) ch. 7; Mircea Eliade, *Myth and Reality* (New York: Harper and Row, 1963) ch. 1; Fawcett, ch. 6. On myth in the Old and New Testatment, see for example, John L. McKenzie, *Myths and Realities* (Milwaukee: Bruce Publishing Company, 1963) chs. 8 and 9; James P. Mackey, *Jesus, the Man and the Myth* (New York: Paulist Press, 1979).

[43] See Eliade, *Patterns*, ch. 12. From a somewhat different perspective, see Joseph Campbell, *Myths to Live By* (New York: Viking Press, 1972) and *The Hero With a Thousand Faces* (Cleveland: World Publishing Company, 1956).

It is important to emphasize that primitive and ancient myths were not imaginative stories devised to "cover up" human ignorance or to "fill in the gaps" between the few things that people knew about themselves and their world. Rather they were symbolic expressions of what people actually *did* understand about life, its meaning, and how it is to be lived. Behind every myth there stands an insight that some individual or society in the past has had into the nature of reality, into the meaning of life, and into the value of thinking and behaving in certain ways. The myths of different religions sometimes vary greatly in what they say (the content of the insight) and in how they say it (the symbolic language or story used to express it), and so we can distinguish between the Judeo-Christian myths and those of other religions. But at the level of archetypal patterns the form and function of myths in all religions seem to be similar: they offer paradigms or models of the way things are, or of the way things ought to be, or of the way things should be done. In Eliade's words, "The foremost function of myth is to reveal explanatory models for all human rites and all significant human actions — diet or marriage, work or education, art or wisdom."[44]

It is on this basis, then, that primitive peoples distinguish truth from falsity in their symbolic stories. Any story which describes the correct way to do things, which portrays the right way to live, or which displays the proper values and attitudes is "true." Conversely, any story which departs from these norms is "false" to a greater or lesser degree. In this perspective, tales which say that hunters are (or should be) brave and that children always (or should always) respect their parents are "true," whereas tales which suggest the opposite are "false." From this same perspective, though at a slightly higher level of generalization, both of the creation stories in the book of Genesis are "true" because they correctly describe human beings' relation to God and nature, even though in the first account man and woman are

---

[44] Eliade, *Myth and Reality*, p. 8; see also *Patterns*, pp. 410, 419, 425-27, 430.

created last, and in the second account man is created first among the inhabitants of earth and woman is created last.

What has just been said of myth, which is symbolic narrative, can also be said of ritual, which is symbolic action. Although it is generally conceded that ritual developed before myth, and that myths are to some extent a spelling out in words what rituals depict in actions,[45] it is often easier for us today to understand the meaning of a ritual by relating it to the myth which is its verbal expression. Perhaps at an earlier stage of human evolution all that was needed was the repetition of the "true" action for individuals to feel and enter into its "truth," but in all known religions (including Christianity) the significance of rituals is narrated in myths and the significance of myths is acted out in rituals. In fact, it is often through ritual that religious people enter into the symbolic world of the myth and experience its deep significance for their lives. What Eliade describes in the context of tribal religions is analogously true of all religions, including our own:

> "Living" a myth, then, implies a genuinely "religious" experience, since it differs from the ordinary experience of everyday life. The "religiousness" of this experience is due to the fact that one re-enacts fabulous, exalting, significant events, once again witnessing the creative deeds of the Supernaturals; one ceases to exist in the everyday world and enters a transfigured, auroral world impregnated with the Supernaturals' presence. What is involved is not a commemoration of mythical events but a reiteration of them."[46]

It is primarily through symbols, therefore, that people express what they have experienced in the world of the sacred and communicate that experience to others. Some-

---

[45] See Louis Bouyer, *Rite and Man* (Notre Dame, Indiana: University of Notre Dame Press, 1963) chs. 4 and 5, and esp. p. 73; also Adolf E. Jensen, *Myth and Cult Among Primitive Peoples* (Chicago: University of Chicago Press, 1963) esp. pp. 39-45.

[46] Eliade, *Myth and Reality*, p. 19.

times particular symbols are so tied to particular individuals and societies that what "says" the sacred for them does not say anything to others. There are, however, archetypal symbols which seem to be able to mediate experiences of the sacred in many different cultures, partly because while their surface meaning is peculiar to each religion their depth meaning is common to human beings no matter where and when they live.

In some way, all symbols "image" the reality that they call to mind or make psychologically present to us. Such images can be natural objects or simple diagrams which appear to be filled with mana. More frequently the images are complex: either the complex stories narrated in myths, or the complex activities performed in rituals. Sometimes the same encounter with the sacred is expressed in both myth and ritual, and so the same mystery is revealed through both. Moreover, both myth and ritual are judged to be true or false according to whether or not they represent the right way to live, the way that is disclosed in the world of the sacred.

4. *The Ritual Dimension*

In the mid-1960s Erik Erikson developed a theory about the psychological importance of ritual and the sequential development of the various elements that are found in adult rituals.[47] Although this theory is not as well known as his theory of the eight stages of human development,[48] it is of particular interest for understanding the role of ritual in

---

[47]See Erik H. Erikson, "The Development of Ritualization" in *The Religious Situation, 1968* edited by Donald R. Cutler (Boston: Beacon Press, 1968) pp. 711-733. This theory is at the core of his *Toys and Reasons: Stages in the Ritualization of Experience* (New York: W. W. Norton and Company, 1977). His ideas have also been applied to the sacraments by George Worgul in the work cited above, pp. 52-62.

[48]For a clear summary, see Erik H. Erikson, *Childhood and Society* (New York: W. W. Norton and Company, 2nd ed. 1963) ch. 7.

psychological development and the contribution that each stage makes to the experience of ritual in adulthood.

Envision, if you will, the interactions between mother and infant. He cries, and she comes to him. She cares for his needs, overcoming the nameless feeling of aloneness that threatens to engulf him. He responds with trust that expresses itself in a calm relaxation. She smiles; he gradually recognizes the source of his comfort, and learns to smile back. "The encounter of the maternal person and small infant, an encounter which is one of mutual trustworthiness and mutual recognition... is the first experience of what in later reoccurrences in love and admiration can only be called a sense of "hallowed presence," the need for which remains basic in man."[49] It is in infancy that we first need to find a sacred "other," and it is through responding to our mother's affection that we both develop the capacity to perceive other people as able to be trusted and loved, and we develop the ability to sense the sacred presence of God in religious worship. For the first important element in religious ritual is a sense of the sacred.

The second stage of ritualization in human development may be called the "judicial" stage because during it we learn to judge between right and wrong at a very basic level. During early childhood we are repeatedly told what is "good" and "bad," and we learn to distinguish the two partly by learning and repeating socially approved behavior and by ritualistically avoiding actions which are not acceptable to our parents and others. In other words, in early childhood we learn how to behave in public and we accept that doing things with people means conforming to certain rules. Through such ritualization, then, we both develop the capacity to interact with others in ways that our society accepts as normal, and we develop the ability to sense what is appropriate and inappropriate behavior in religious worship. For the second important element in religious ritual is the sense that this is the proper thing to do.

---

[49]Erik H. Erikson, *Identity: Youth and Crisis* (New York: W. W. Norton and Company, 1968) p. 105.

The third stage of everyday ritualization may be called the "dramatic" stage because at this point in our lives we first develop the ability to see sequences of events as little dramas with a beginning, middle and end. Pre-school children play with dolls and doll houses, building-block villages and their inhabitants, cars and trucks, and in doing so they also create miniature plays in which people and objects interact with each other in appropriate patterns. Children at this age also play at roles, pretending to be mommy and daddy, cowboy and cowgirl, nurse and fireman, modeling their dramatic actions on what they perceive as adult roles and interactions. Through these little rituals, therefore, we both develop the ability to cooperate with other persons through more prolonged periods of social interaction, and we develop the capacity to perceive human rituals as dramatic wholes, whether those rituals be ballets or sporting events, operas or plays, Bible services or Eucharistic liturgies. For the third main element in religious ritual is its form as drama, having a period of preparation, a moment of climax, and a period of coming to completion.

The fourth stage of ritualization in our ordinary experience may be called the "formal" stage because through it we come to appreciate the perfection of performance in the things that we do by ourselves or with others. During our years at school, for example, "play is transformed into work, game into cooperation, and the freedom of the imagination into the duty to perform with full attention to all the minute details which are necessary to complete a task and do it 'right'."[50] The human need to develop through ritualization at this age is met by the gradual mastery of school subjects and musical instruments, by participating in team sports and practicing until it's perfect, by joining youth organizations and earning awards for the acquisition of new skills. Through such ritual devotion to formal tasks we develop the ability to attend to and delight in the fine details of activity, and we develop the capacity to focus on, perform and appreciate the external and internal intricacies of ritual

[50]Erikson in *The Religious Situation, 1968,* p. 726f.

worship. For the fourth main element in religious ritual is its character of being formal or stylized behavior.

If the formal aspect of ritual is insisted upon but the ceremony (whether it be secular or religious) does not arouse a sense of the sacred, is not perceived as the right thing to do, or loses its dramatic integrity, it can appear as empty formalism. This is especially true for adolescents, for whom the fifth stage of ritualization brings a demand for solidarity of conviction. At this stage of self-identification and social commitment the rituals learned in childhood need to be accepted as one's own and integrated into one's identity as a member of the social group from whom they were learned. It is through the performance of rituals during adolescence, therefore, that we add our own assent and approval to what we have become in the preceding stages of our development. In this way we become able to perform civil ceremonies and religious rituals with conviction, that is, we recognize them as symbolizing what we believe and value, and we identify with what the symbols stand for. For the fifth principal element in religious ritual is the sense that this symbolic action is both "mine" and "ours," plus the affirmation that what it signifies is real and worthwhile.

It is important to remember that according to this theory of sequential development, while each stage builds on the accomplishments of the preceding stages, the accomplishments of those stages are retained in the more developed ritualization of the later stages.

> Man's epigenetic development in separate and protracted childhood stages assures that each of the major elements which constitute human institutions [whether they be everyday rituals or specifically ceremonial rituals] is rooted in a distinct childhood stage, but, once evolved, must be progressively reintegrated on each higher level.[51]

Nevertheless, Erikson believes that by adolescence all of the psychologically important elements of ritual have been

---

[51]Same, p. 725.

developed in each person. But what then of adulthood? Doesn't this stage of human growth contribute something to the development of ritual? Erikson believes not, and instead he suggests that "a dominant function of ritual in the life of the adult" meets a "need to be periodically reinforced in his role of ritualizer" for the younger generation.[52] In Erikson's overall theory of human development, the primary task of the adult years is generativity, which encompasses both biological creativity and social accomplishment, and he envisages adult participation in ritual as a means of accomplishing this generative task of passing on one's personal and cultural achievements to others.

This does not imply, however, that developmental psychology can offer nothing more to our understanding of religious ritual. For one thing, if it is true that the accomplishments of each lower stage of personal development are retained as one grows through the later stages, then liturgy and worship can both reaffirm those accomplishments and reinforce them in addition to encouraging them in those who have not yet suceeded in doing so. Erikson himself suggests this when he says that religion is "the institution which throughout man's history has striven to verify basic trust," which is the foundation for all further human development.[53] Certainly baptism and Eucharist, for example, can be seen as both affirming and enabling the development of trusting relationships among members of the Church and between individuals and God. Confirmation may be viewed as a celebration of autonomy and initiative in Christian living (Erikson's stages two and three) as well as an encouragement towards greater activity within and identification with the Church (stages four and five). Penance can be at least one means of effecting reconciliation between persons and between individuals and God, and so bring about a greater measure of intimacy (stage six) in human living. Both marriage and ordination are celebrations of generativ-

[52]Same, pp. 729, 730 (italics deleted).
[53]Erikson, *Identity: Youth and Crisis*, p. 106.

ity in human living (stage seven). And the anointing of the sick can help those in later years to perceive the fundamental integrity of their lives within a Christian perspective (stage eight).[54]

For another thing, Erikson's developmental theories are not the only ones in psychology, and there are others which trace other dimensions of human development or which explore other areas of human experience and living.[55] So although Erikson offers us a model for the development of ritualization, his work certainly does not fully explore the psychological richness of sacramental rituals. Some of that richness is discussed in the further volumes on the sacraments and sacramentals in this series.[56] Here we shall have to be content with reviewing some of the other psychological aspects of religious ritual in general.

In the preceding section on symbolism we looked primarily at symbols as *expressions* of religious experience, although we also saw how through association with basic human emotions and ideas symbols can also make a deep *impression* on people. This is just another way of saying that symbols can be causes of hierophanies, and it turns out that in the history of religions most symbols that give rise to hierophanies occur in the context of rituals. How then do rituals make the impression that they make on people? How do they occasion hierophanies that occur in sacred space and time?

This is a complex matter that we are only now beginning to understand, but Victor Turner has discovered that most religious rituals take place in a situation of "liminality" or

---

[54]On this latter point, see in this series, James L. Empereur, S.J., *Prophetic Anointing* (Wilmington, Delaware: Michael Glazier, 1982) pp. 159-181.

[55]See Jean Piaget, *Genetic Epistemology* (New York: Columbia University Press, 1970), and *The Child and Reality* (New York: Viking Press, 1973); Lawrence Kohlberg, *The Philosophy of Moral Development* (San Francisco: Harper and Row, 1981); James Fowler, *Stages of Faith* (San Francisco: Harper and Row, 1981).

[56]For further direct applications of developmental psychology to sacramental instruction, consult the director's guidelines and/or scope and sequence charts for the religious education programs of the major Catholic catechetical publishers.

in-between-ness. This is most clear in the case of so-called "rites of passage" or rituals which bring about a transition from one state in life to another (for example, puberty rites in tribal religion, ordination to the priesthood in Catholicism, and marriage ceremonies in either) but it is also found to a greater or lesser degree in all religious worship and sacramental ceremony, and it is even found outside the context of religion. Liminality may be described as a condition of being outside a social group, of being on the fringe of a certain social structure, or of being in-between and in transition from one social group or structure to another. Psychologically it is a condition of feeling neither here nor there in the standard social order. To some extent adolescents have this feeling naturally, for they are in psychological and social transition from childhood to adulthood. Artists, intellectuals and social critics are also often liminal individuals both in regard to their social standing and in regard to their own psychological attitude. It is important to recognize, however, that we all go through liminal periods in our lives (not only adolescence but also courtship, illness, graduation, career change, relocation, etc.) during which our normal ways of behaving and looking at life come a little unglued. Psychologically, part of our old perception of reality is disintegrating or is in suspension, and we are open to a new integration, a new vision of reality.

What happens in religious rituals, then, is something akin to this phenomenon. It is not something that is automatic, but if we seriously intend to enter into the ritual with our minds and hearts, we leave our ordinary patterns of thinking and feeling behind us. This transition is helped by the entrance procession and preliminary prayers at the beginning of the Eucharistic liturgy, and by analogous periods of preparation as we enter into other types of worship. To talk about it in terms that we have already met, we enter the world of the sacred, but here we notice that this world for most of us is a liminal world in the sense of being marginal, because for most of us it exists on the edges of our practical life. It is also liminal in the sense of being in-between, because we come into it out of our profane world of everyday concerns and a little later we return from it to that same profane world. While we are in that liminal realm of experience, however, the ordinary pragmatic ways of thinking and feeling are temporarily suspended, and we find ourselves open to those ideas and values that are presented to us through the symbols of the sacramental liturgy (including the linguistic symbols of the prayers, readings and homily).[57]

That religious experience is characterized by liminality comes as no surprise once we recognize that Moses and the prophets, Jesus and the apostles, and indeed most charismatic religious leaders were liminal figures *vis-a-vis* the established social structures of their day. Moreover, their followers were often either social outcasts (like Mary Magdalene) or willing to question the established view of things (like Joseph of Arimathea). But as Turner points out, people who share the same liminal experience often develop a psychic bond between them which he calls "communitas," which Catholic writers tend to call community or spiritual unity, and which Protestant writers sometimes call fellowship or oneness. As an experience, however, communitas is not unique to religion, for the experience of togetherness is also found in families, among the poor and oppressed, among beatniks and hippies, and among victims of natural disasters, to mention but a few instances. It is an experience of commonality and togetherness that disregards the differences that social structures impose on people. "The bonds of communitas are anti-structural in the sense that they are undifferentiated, equalitarian, direct, extant, nonrational, existential, I-Thou ... relationships."[58]

Moslem pilgrims to Mecca often remark afterwards that

---

[57]When people complain that the Mass or sacraments don't mean anything to them, part of the reason is often that they are psychologically unable (for whatever reason) to fully participate in the ritual by entering into this liminal realm of religious experience.

[58]Turner, *Dramas*, p. 274. On the relation between liminality and communitas, see also *The Ritual Process*, pp. 95-97.

the required wearing of plain white robes which hide any differences of social status or national origin adds immensely to their experience of Islamic unity and deepens their comprehension of the meaning of that brotherhood. To some extent all religious rituals do this, for during them we no longer play our accustomed social roles but instead become together "this parish" or "the Church" or "the people of God." And the fact that we sit and stand together, that we see and hear the same things, and that we sing together and pray in unison — all these symbolically suggest at a depth level that despite our differences we are all united in a common reality.

For all that symbolism, however, the experience of spiritual community is not automatic. As was noted in the section on symbolism, although symbols can express experiences of the sacred, they can in turn be recognized as such only by people who can find in the symbol a representation of what they themselves hold sacred. If they do not see through the symbol to something which is real for them at a depth level — or to say it the other way around, if the symbol does not signify something which they have experienced as true and valuable — then the symbol fails to be effective for them. Applied to the experience of oneness in worship, this means that people can find the unity which all the sacraments (but especially the Eucharist) symbolize only if they have already found it in activities other than worship. As Turner says succinctly, "Communitas in ritual can only be evoked easily when there are many occasions outside the ritual on which communitas has been achieved."[59]

This should not be taken as implying that rituals can have no effect at all on people who have not fully experienced what they symbolize, however. To the extent that they employ archetypal symbols that connect with fundamental needs such as trust, intimacy, generativity or the others that Erikson speaks of, and to the extent that they image basic human values such as fidelity, hope, altruism and so on, to

---

[59]Turner, *Dramas*, p. 56.

that extent they can draw those who are willing to let go of their profane concerns into the realm of the sacred and into the realization that what it discloses is true. Moreover, the fact that rituals are repeated over and over again makes it possible for people to be constantly reminded of what they ought to be experiencing and believing and valuing even when in fact they are not living what their rituals symbolize, and so rituals can to some extent over the course of time engender and shape the very depth realities that they signify.[60]

Rituals are therefore symbolic actions which represent in word and gesture realities which people have already experienced, or may be led to experience. With regard to our everyday experience, it is in fact this latter aspect of ritual which is the more important for, as Erikson has shown, it is through ritualization that we come to experience ourselves as trusting, autonomous and creative persons, and it is through ritualization that we come to know ourselves as members of a social group with definite beliefs and practices. In short, it is through ritualization that in many ways we come to be what we are, both individually and socially.

With regard to religious experience, however, it is the former aspect of ritual which is the more important, for it is in these special rituals, set apart from the rituals of everyday life, that we express and find expressed the beliefs and practices, values and ideals of our everyday rituals. As Turner has shown, these rituals often entail experiences of liminality not only because they sometimes occur at transition points in our lives but also because they are in fact special and thus set apart from our ordinary routines. In such rituals we find symbolized many of the deepest realities that we experience every day, in a bond of communitas with others who share that same experience and acknowledge those same realities. But such rituals also give us the opportunity to perceive ideas and ideals that we have perhaps lost sight of and are not fully enacting in our lives. In religious rituals such as the sacraments, then, we see what we are and

[60]See Worgul, p. 88f.

what we want to become, and we are given the chance to say Yes to it in our heart of hearts.

Recommended Reading

On the psychology of religion:

George Stephens Spinks, *Psychology and Religion: An Introduction to Contemporary Views* (Boston: Beacon Press, 1967) despite its subtitle discusses only the classical approaches to the subject, but does this quite thoroughly.

Robert H. Thouless, *An Introduction to the Psychology of Religion* (London: Cambridge University Press, 3rd edition 1971) covers both the classical and behaviorist approaches in concise, well written chapters, even though it does not specifically discuss the psychological aspects of symbol and ritual.

Geoffrey E. W. Scobie, *Psychology of Religion* (New York: John Wiley and Sons, 1975) contains a compact and fairly up-to-date survey of the field.

Abraham H. Maslow, *Religions, Values and Peak Experiences* (New York: Viking Press, 1970) sheds a lot of light on religious experience and the lack of it in Christian rituals, as well as on religious education.

On symbol, myth and ritual:

Ernst Cassirer, *An Essay on Man* (New Haven; Yale University Press, 1944) summarizes many of the ideas that he introduced to the contemporary understanding of symbolism.

Mircea Eliade, *The Sacred and the Profane* (New York: Harcourt Brace and World, 1959) discusses religious myth, symbolism and ritual in terms of sacred space, sacred time and sacred objects. For a more thorough introduction to Eliade's work, read *Myths, Rites, Symbols: A Mircea Eliade Reader* edited by Wendell C. Beane and William G. Doty (New York: Harper and Row, 1975), which contains excerpts from all his major works, arranged by topic.

Thomas Fawcett, *The Symbolic Language of Religion* (Minneapolis: Augsburg Publishing House, 1971) offers a concise yet comprehensive treatment of religious symbolism in Christianity and other religions.

Erik H. Erikson, *Toys and Reasons: Stages in the Ritualization of Experience* (New York: W. W. Norton and Company, 1977) sets his discussion of ritualization in the wider context of individual development and shared visions.

Victor and Edith Turner, *Image and Pilgrimage in Christian Culture* (New York: Columbia University Press, 1978) applies his analysis of ritual and symbol to certain aspects of Christianity, and has a valuable appendix summarizing the main elements in that analysis.

CHAPTER II: SOCIOLOGY AND THE SACRAMENTS

Sacraments are not just for individuals. In fact there is not one of them that can be performed alone.[1] Sacraments are group actions, and under normal conditions they involve a number of persons in dramatic interaction with one another. The participants do or say things to each other and their ritual action simultaneously speaks to those others who observe it. Sacraments are also group actions in the sense that they are stylized behaviors developed by religious communities which both signify something important about the group and make it to be what it is.

1. Social Dimensions of the Sacraments

For a long time the communal and ecclesial aspects of the sacraments were so taken for granted that they were largely overlooked by theology even though they were never entirely forgotten. Medieval theology paid close attention to the minister and recipient of each sacrament, and discussions about sacramental effects were pretty much confined

---

[1] Even the "private Mass" of medieval and modern times, said by a priest without congregation present, was offered in the name of the Church and usually on behalf of someone else besides the celebrant.

to talking about those received by individual souls.[2] Early modern sacramental piety likewise focused on the importance of the sacraments for individual growth towards God and ultimate salvation in heaven.[3] It was mainly in canon law that the sacraments were viewed as vital for the institutional life of the Church, and so their proper performance was duly regulated and their ecclesiastical consequences were thought out in some detail.[4]

Starting in the nineteenth century, however, the liturgical movement tried to deepen the Catholic understanding of the sacraments by examining their historical development.[5] One of its first discoveries was that during the patristic period, congregations did not passively watch but actively participated in the Mass. Later it learned how the whole community had once been involved in the celebration of baptism and penance, sacraments which in the Middle Ages had become private affairs between a minister and a recipient. But the real interests of the movement were not antiquarian but practical, and so cautiously at first it proposed such radical innovations (for that time) as allowing people to use missals and encouraging them to sing Gregorian chant. Eventually this gradual reintroduction of lay participation in Catholic worship led to an increasing awareness that all of the sacraments did have a communal dimension which ought to be better reflected in the rites themselves. By this time, Vatican II was only a step away.[6]

[2]For a summary of the traditional theology of each of the sacraments, see the articles in the *New Catholic Encyclopedia* (New York: McGraw Hill, 1966) under "Sacraments, Theology of" and under the names of the individual sacraments.

[3]See, for example, A.-M. Roguet, *Christ Acts Through The Sacraments* (Collegeville, Minnesota: Liturgical Press, 1954).

[4]Before Vatican II the sacraments were often treated within moral theology, and moral theology was in large measure governed by canon law. For an example of this, see Dominic Prummer, O.P., *Handbook of Moral Theology* (New York: P.J. Kenedy and Sons, 1957) Part Two.

[5]See the essays collected in *The Liturgical Movement* (New York: Hawthorn Books, 1964), and *Liturgy in Development* (Westminster, Maryland: Newman Press, 1966).

[6]Significantly, the first document promulgated by the bishops at the Council was the *Constitution on the Sacred Liturgy* (Dec. 4, 1963), and it emphasized "active participation" in Catholic worship.

In the middle of the twentieth century the liturgical movement gained added impetus from the scriptural movement in the Church.[7] When Pope Pius XII in his encyclical *Divino Afflante Spiritu* instructed Catholic scholars to begin using modern methods of scientific research to develop a better understanding of the Bible, they were able to show how in many ways the New Testament was a product of the early Christian community and not just the work of individual writers. Many gospel passages, for example, show evidence of having been used in community worship before being written down and collected. And the same is true of what we now recognize as early hymns in the letters of St. Paul. A better understanding of the Old Testament too revealed how Jewish worship was intrinsically communal, and it suggested that if the Church is truly the new Israel then the Catholic liturgy should not be an opportunity for private prayer but an occasion in which the people of God assemble for common prayer.

These advances in liturgical and scriptural scholarship in turn led systematic theologians to rethink the meaning and function of the Mass and the sacraments in the Catholic life of worship. After the introduction of the notion of "the Church as sacrament" by Otto Semmelroth and others in the 1950s,[8] a number of theologians strove to find a social aspect in each of the seven sacraments and to integrate it within the traditional framework of sacramental theology.[9] Eventually, however, Catholic thinkers began to abandon scholastic philosophy in favor of more contemporary intellectual frameworks, and once they did this, the social dimension of the sacraments began to be appreciated even

---

[7]For a good introduction to the renewal of Catholic scripture studies, see Raymond E. Brown, S.S., *New Testament Essays* (Milwaukee: Bruce Publishing Company, 1965) ch. 1.

[8]Otto Semmelroth, S.J., *Church and Sacrament* (Notre Dame, Indiana: Fides Publishers, 1965) was originally published in German in 1953. Likewise, Edward Schillebeeckx, whose seminal works were not translated into English until the following decade, was being published in Europe during this period.

[9]See, for example, Bernard Leeming, S.J., *Principles of Sacramental Theology* (London: Longmans, Green and Company, 1956) ch. 11; Karl Rahner, S.J., *The Church and the Sacraments* (New York: Herder and Herder, 1963) Part II.

more.[10] Today in academic, pastoral and catechetical treatments of the sacraments, their intrinsically social nature is both recognized and emphasized.[11]

2. The Functional Dimension

Until relatively recently in the history of the human race, the social worlds that people grew up in were dominated by a very few social institutions, namely their family, their religion and their government.[12] These social institutions are still around, but they are not the only important ones any more. Today there are peer groups, social and political organizations, educational institutions and mass media all vying for our attention and our allegiance. Morever, they are perceived as different from each other and the traditional three, partly because they do not all say or stand for the same things. Traditionally (which here means for thousands, even hundreds of thousands of years) family, religion and government all stood for the same basic beliefs and values. Together they supported one another, the social structure in which they were enmeshed, and the individuals who grew up within that social structure.[13]

Today the situation is much different. For instance, the role that religion plays in introducing individuals to social realities is much smaller than it used to be. Nevertheless it is still important. For one thing, although religion is not a part

[10]See George McCauley, S.J., *Sacraments for Secular Man* (New York: Herder and Herder, 1969); Bernard Haring, C.SS.R., *The Sacraments and Your Everyday Life* (Liguori, Missouri: Liguori Publications, 1976).

[11]See George S. Worgul, Jr., *From Magic to Metaphor* (New York: Paulist Press, 1980) esp. ch. 5; William Bausch, *A New Look at the Sacraments*, Second Edition, (Notre Dame, Indiana: Fides/Claretian, 1983); Tad Guzie, *The Book of Sacramental Basics* (New York: Paulist Press, 1981).

[12]In small primitive societies these three are even often united into one: the tribe or clan.

[13]See Peter Berger and Thomas Luckman, *The Social Construction of Reality* (New York: Doubleday, 1966); also Gerhard Lenski, *The Religious Factor* (New York: Doubleday, 1961). For a more general perspective, see Peter Berger, *Invitation to Sociology* (New York: Doubleday, 1963).

of education and government as it once was, it is still an element in family life, and the first world that children grow up in is the home. For another thing, the subjects taught in school are supposed to be "value free" (or at least "value neutral"), government is no longer perceived as the guardian of national virtues, and the values proposed through the mass media are conflicting at best. Therefore, although we cannot even say that religion is important in everyone's life, helping them to develop a sense of what is true and valuable, we can say that when it is important to people it does perform some important social functions.[14]

Early anthropologists and sociologists sometimes defined religion in terms of its psychological or cognitive aspects: the experience of the sacred or the acceptance of beliefs about transcendent realities.[15] Others preferred to focus on the structural elements in religion, such as myth, ritual and hierarchical leadership.[16] Since the 1950s, however, many sociologists following Talcott Parsons' theory of structural functionalism have focused on the various functions that religion performs for individuals and societies.[17] Such func-

---

[14]See Elizabeth K. Nottingham, *Religion: A Sociological View* (New York: Random House, 1971) p. 44f.

[15]For example, in his *Sociology of Religion* (Chicago: University of Chicago Press, 1944) p. 13, Joachim Wach approvingly quotes Rudolf Otto's definition that "Religion is the experience of the Holy."

[16]For example, Emile Durkheim in 1912 defined religion as "a unified system of beliefs and practices relative to sacred things, that is to say, things set apart and forbidden — beliefs and practices which unite into one single moral community called a Church." *The Elementary Forms of the Religious Life* (New York: The Free Press, 1962) p. 62.

[17]According to J. Milton Yinger, religion "can be defined as a system of beliefs and practices by means of which a group of people struggles with these ultimate problems of human life" such as death, suffering, and existence itself. *The Scientific Study of Religion* (New York: Macmillan, 1970) p. 7. For an overview of Parsons' structural functionalism, see Jonathan H. Turner, *The Structure of Sociological Theory* (Homewood, Illinois: The Dorsey Press, 1974) ch. 3. For an extensive application of structural functionalism to religion, see Louis Schneider, *Sociological Approach to Religion* (New York: John Wiley and Sons, 1970) chs. 3-5. And for a summary history of sociological attempts to define religion, see P.H. Vrijhof, "What is the Sociology of Religion?" in Joan Brothers, ed., *Readings in the Sociology of Religion* (New York: Pergamon Press, 1967) pp. 38-50.

tions include providing a meaning of life, legitimizing the existing social structure, maintaining a code of morality, and explaining the ultimate nature of reality.

Thomas O'Dea has grouped the functions of religion under six main headings.[18] First, religion "provides *support, consolation* and *reconciliation*" to people when they are faced with uncertainty, confronted with disappointment, and alienated from each other or from society as a whole. Second, "religion offers a *transcendental relationship* through cult and the ceremonies of worship" to a divine being and even to other human beings, giving people a greater sense of security and stability amidst the flux and changes of life. Third, "religion *sacralizes the norms and values* of established societies" by placing them within a divinely revealed moral code, but it also provides ways that individuals who violate those sacred norms can overcome their own guilt and be forgiven by others. Fourth, religion also has "the *prophetic* function" of holding forth ideals "in terms of which institutionalized norms may be critically examined and found seriously wanting." Fifth, "religion performs important *identity* functions," helping people to situate themselves in the cosmos and in society, giving them a sense of who they are and what they are supposed to be. Sixth, "religion is related to the growth and maturation of the individual," guiding his or her passage through the various stages of human development and various changes in social position. According to the functionalist view, therefore, the primary functions of religion are integrative, since it aids the integration of the individual within society and also the self-integration of the individual in terms of self-knowledge, self-identity and self-acceptance. But religion also has an innovative function, since besides maintaining the established order it can also criticize and transform social institutions and individual habits.

One of the principal ways that religion performs these

---

[18]See Thomas F. O'Dea, *The Sociology of Religion* (Englewood Cliffs, New Jersey: Prentice Hall, 1966) pp. 13-16. All of the following quotations are from those pages.

various functions is through the use of symbols. The primary symbols in any religion are archetypal paradigms which reveal the hidden meaning of life and clarify the mysterious nature of the universe. In Mircea Eliade's words, "The symbol reveals certain aspects of reality — the deepest aspects — which defy any other means of knowledge."[19] For Christians the primary symbol is the life, death and resurrection of Jesus Christ, which is the ultimate revelation of the mystery of God and the definitive exemplar of how we are to live out the mystery in our own attitudes and actions. The same is true to a greater or lesser extent of the rest of revelation, in both scripture and tradition. "Christian truth is symbolic," says sociologist and theologian Gregory Baum, because it "reveals the hidden structure of human life and by doing so significantly transforms the self understanding of those who receive it."[20] The human imagination is not fixed; people are not born with a set of *a priori* ideas about reality or thought forms through which they interpret their experience. The wide diversity of cultures and religions past and present bears adequate testimony to this. Rather, "experience has a structure in which the symbols governing the imagination have a creative part," and so people's response to the world is in large measure "determined by the symbols operative in their imagination." In other words, the function of these symbols is to "define the vision of life out of which people operate and thus orient their actions in a certain direction."[21]

As we have already noted in the previous chapter, symbols not only express religious beliefs and attitudes, but they are also a means through which people learn about them and reaffirm them. Thus for Christians, "if symbols reveal the divine presence in the universe, then their assimilation in

---

[19] Mircea Eliade, *Images and Symbols* (New York: Sheed and Ward, 1961) p. 12. Likewise Paul Tillich: The symbol "opens up levels of reality which are otherwise closed for us." *Dynamics of Faith* (New York: Harper and Row, 1958) p. 42.

[20] Gregory Baum, *Religion and Alienation* (New York: Paulist Press, 1975) p. 241.

[21] Same, p. 242.

the imagination will make people follow the divine will and lead them on the way of salvation."[22] But this internalization of the symbolic truths of faith happens primarily in and through the Church, by active participation in the believing community. There Christians "share life with people enjoying the same vision. There they are surrounded by the signs of faith. There they listen to the scriptures, celebrate the liturgy and study Christian teaching."[23] In and through the Church they learn to live the Christian myth, if you will, by assimilating into their imagination the fundamental structures of reality that are disclosed in the scriptures and the person of Jesus, and by incorporating into their lives the pattern of attitudes and actions that is congruent with that reality.

Archetypal symbols are found not only in the language of myth, however, but also in the gestures and objects used in ritual. Functionally speaking, rituals are "repetitive activities that provide a sense of participation in the mythic framework" of any given religion.[24] Most religious rituals are cultic actions, stylized activities set apart from the routine of everyday living, in which the religious group conceives and enacts its sacred meanings and values. It conceives them in myth and it enacts them in ritual; thus myth and ritual are correlative and inseparable. To say it another way, ritual supplies "ways in which the individual or group may participate in the myth through re-enactment in one form or another."[25]

The roots of religious ritual are to be found in everyday rituals such as those discussed in the previous chapter. Many activities which are patterned by religious ritual in tribal cultures later become secular routines as technology

[22]Same, p. 243f.

[23]Same, p. 246.

[24]Barbara Hargrove, *The Sociology of Religion* (Arlington Heights, Illinois: AHM Publishing Corporation, 1979) p. 11.

[25]Same, p. 10. See also, Aidan Kavanaugh, "The Role of Ritual in Personal Development" in James D. Shaughnessy, ed., *The Roots of Ritual* (Grand Rapids, Michigan: William B. Eerdmans, 1971) p. 148f.

develops: hunting, farming, tool making, house building, and so on. Initially, such technological breakthroughs are sacred in the sense that they are terribly important for the survival and well being of the group. Their importance is illustrated in mythic stories, and knowledge of them is communicated from one generation to the next through periodically repeated rituals: hunting dances, fertility rites, house building ceremonies, and the like.[26] In the geographically limited tribal society the rituals dramatize, as far as anyone in that society can see, "how human beings do this," and the myths narrate "how people came to know this" or explain "how this fits into the overall pattern of human living." In a very real sense, therefore, primitive peoples learn how to be human by learning and then living the patterns of behavior that are preserved and handed down through ritual. Early human rituals encompass not only the technological routines mentioned here but virtually all cultural activities (sharing food, coping with illness, making agreements, waging war, etc.) and social relationships (parents and children, in-laws and outcasts, rulers and subjects, etc.). And although in the course of time many of these rituals become so commonplace that they are no longer religious, their sacredness is still preserved in the attitudes which regard them as "the right way to do things," the unquestioned rules of custom and etiquette, or "the tradition of which we are proud."

As the sacred rituals needed for survival and civilized living become profane routines, therefore, specifically religious rituals tend to be reserved for those dimensions of life which are still imbued with mystery (for example, birth, growth, sex, sickness, death), those aspects of reality which are still not fully comprehended (for example, the cycles of the seasons, the weather, natural catastrophes, the experience of the supernatural), and those elements of culture which are regarded as ultimately important (for example,

---

[26]See Wach, p. 41. The classic treatment of this phenomenon is found in Branislaw Malinowski's 1925 essay, *Magic, Science and Religion* (New York: Doubleday Anchor Books, 1954) esp. ch. 2.

authority, family relationships, national origins, memorable persons and events of the past). These rituals dramatize ideas and values which the group holds in common and which hold the group itself together: "Ritual is perhaps the strongest nonbiological bond that unites people into a functioning social unit."[27] Participation in religious rituals can raise consciousness to a state of heightened awareness of ideas and values, which not only reinforces those attitudes but also deepens the commitment of people to those others who share them.[28]

In summary, then, religion — and specifically religious myth and ritual — performs a number of important social functions. In an increasingly secularized society many of these functions can get taken over by nonreligious ideologies and purely cultural rituals, either for a large minority or even for a majority of individuals. But for religious persons (and we are speaking here not about mere churchgoers but about persons who are deeply committed to what their religious symbols represent) many if not most of these functions are performed by many if not most of their religious activities (which is not to say that such people do not have secular commitments as well). For Catholics this means that consciously and deliberately participating in the Eucharistic liturgy and other sacraments does much more than fulfill external religious obligations. Through these rituals (although these are not the only ways it happens) we both express our inner commitment to the Christian way of life and we interiorize the ideas and values, beliefs and attitudes which are congruent with the Christian revelation. Expressed theologically rather than sociologically, we put on the mind of Christ, become one with our Lord, and build up his body, which is the Church.

---

[27]Hargrove, p. 79.

[28]See O'Dea, pp. 39-41. For a summary of the classical analyses of ritual, see S.P. Nagendra, *The Concept of Ritual in Modern Sociological Theory* (New Delhi: The Academic Journals of India, 1971).

3. The Effective Dimension

Closely allied to the functional dimension of religion is the effective dimension of religious ritual, which is just another way of saying that rituals can and do affect people. They effect alterations in their attitudes and changes in their lives. Traditional theology spoke of sacraments as effective signs, but it analyzed their effectiveness using metaphysical concepts such as instrumental causality. Today we no longer think in terms of metaphysical causality, but we can still recognize the phenomenon of sacramental effectiveness. And now we can speak of it in other terms as well.[29] Using the techniques of linguistic analysis we can examine the types and levels of sacramental language. Anthropology and comparative religion can give us insights into the impact of myth and ritual on religious peoples everywhere. Depth psychology can shed light on the nature of religious experience and the effects of religious symbolism. And we can use sociological concepts for understanding the social dynamics of religion and ritual.[30]

Yet speaking about the sacraments in psychological and sociological terms can sometimes be disconcerting and even seem disrespectful. One reason for this is that throughout our history as a church we have focused on the sacraments' theological effects: by baptism we are freed from sin and incorporated into Christ, by confirmation we are spiritually strengthened by the Holy Spirit, in the Eucharist we become

---

[29] The shift from metaphysical to sociological categories of thought among religious thinkers is simply a matter of history and culture; it does not imply that the philosophical approach is any less true than approaches based on the other social sciences. For contemporary attempts to understand the sacraments using various philosophical categories, see Chapter IV of this work.

[30] For an attempt to examine traditional Catholic claims about the sacraments using concepts from the social sciences, see B.R. Brinkman, "On Sacramental Man," a series of articles in *The Heythrop Journal*: "I, Language Patterning" 13(1972)371-401; "II, The Way of Intimacy" 14(1973)5-34; "III, The Socially Operational Way" 14(1973)162-189; "IV, The Way of Interiorization" 14(1973)280-306; "V, The Way of Sacramental Operationalism" 14(1973)396-416. A number of Brinkman's ideas are summarized in the work by Worgul cited above, pp. 79-92 passim.

united to Christ, through penance our sins are forgiven, and so on. These may be called the intended effects of the sacraments, for they reflect what the minister and recipient of the sacrament have in mind when participating in the sacramental ceremony, and they reflect the meaning of the words and gestures that compose the rite itself. When we think about our experience of sacramental ceremonies, however, and especially when we ponder the multiple effects that they have had on us or others, we begin to realize that there are other unintended but no less real effects of these ceremonies. Among these are the effects that we have discussed in the previous section as functions of religious rituals.[31]

One reason why sacramental actions have multiple effects is, of course, that human beings are complex. We think, we feel, we act, and we interact with others both spontaneously and in culturally established patterns. And so when we participate in sacramental ceremonies we are affected by what we see, hear and do on many different levels. Moreover, the effects can vary in both intensity and duration. And finally, the sacraments can affect us individually and personally, or they can affect us socially and alter our relationships with others, or they can do both.

Until the twentieth century, however, the principal language that theologians had at their disposal for speaking about the effects of the sacraments has been the language of theology, and theological language at least since the Middle Ages drew heavily from the language of scholastic philosophy. As a result, the multiple effects of the sacraments, both psychological and social, tended to get spoken of in philosophical terms such as soul, act and habit, or in theological terms such as grace, character and merit. But today with additional linguistic (and conceptual) tools at our disposal, derived not from medieval philosophy but from the contemporary social sciences, we can analyze sacramental rituals and their effects on us in a greater variety of ways.

---

[31]See also Nottingham, pp.62-64.

We have already seen, for example, that symbolic rituals can have a number of psychological effects. They can be occasions for hierophanies or experiences of the sacred, and through their repetition they can cause the reoccurrence of the experiences that they symbolize. In a very real sense, then, sacraments make God's word and power present to us if we are predisposed to receiving them. Since these hierophanies appear through the symbols, as it were, the experiences take on the structure and meaning of those symbols. Thus the sacraments call to mind events and facts in the life of Christ (for example, the last supper, or his healing ministry), and they can also reawaken or deepen our appreciation of Christian beliefs and values (for example, God's forgiving love, or the importance of self-sacrifice). Rituals thus revitalize ideals and attitudes, but they also promote their initial occurrence in us. Because sacramental rituals can be occasions for the religious experiences that they symbolize, during the liturgy and other sacramental ceremonies we are more prone to feel at one with God and others, to have our conscience disturbed, to have our anxieties calmed, and to pray in any number of ways. Finally, some rituals represent reasons for joy and celebration, and so participating in sacramental worship can also give us feelings of festivity.

Psychologically, however, it is unlikely that we would feel much festivity if we were alone in our ritual, and so it becomes apparent that many of the psychological effects of the sacraments are tied up with their social aspects. And although there are a number of ways to discuss the sociological effects of rituals,[32] we may for the purpose of convenience divide them into three categories: unification, transition and communication.

First and foremost, then, rituals have a unifying effect on those who participate in them. Performing a common ritual with others (even though not all the performers have the same function in the ritual) unites people in a common action. Rituals therefore have an inherent power to say to

---

[32]For a rather comprehensive treatment of this, see Anthony F.C. Wallace, *Religion, An Anthropological View* (New York: Random House, 1966) chs. 3-5.

people, "We're in this together," for that is precisely what is happening on the level of physical behavior. It renews their identity within a religious group, and it creates a sense of solidarity with the other members. In our religious experience as Catholics this occurs most frequently during the Eucharistic liturgy, not only because it is the one sacramental ritual which regularly brings us together as a community, but also because its central symbol is one of communion. Moreover, being together in the same religious ritual heightens people's awareness of common beliefs and values, deepens their appreciation for them, and intensifies their commitment to common ways of thinking and behaving.[33] No matter which sacrament we participate in, we have a sense that this is what we all believe in, this is what is important, and this is the right thing to do. Finally, in the symbolic drama of ritual people see a pattern of living which is appropriate not only for the present but also for the future. And so through the sacraments we learn not only how to behave during the ceremonies but also how to relate to God, to ourselves, and to others in our lives as Christians.[34]

In a discussion such as this, however, it must also be remembered that the psycho-sociological effects of the sacraments basically reflect and intensify the felt social realities of the celebrating group (though they can also to some extent engender and communicate them, as we shall see in a while). For example, if there is no sense of unity among people in a parish before they come to Sunday worship, it cannot be reflected in the Mass. And if there are not shared commitments to common values and ideals, they cannot be intensified in liturgical worship. More generally and somewhat more accurately, we can say that to the extent that these realities are present or lacking in any given group, to

---

[33] On this point, see Michael G. Lawler, "Christian Rituals: An Essay in Sacramental Symbolism," *Horizons* 7(1980) pp. 8, 13, 32.

[34] On sacraments as a means of entering into the realm of properly Christian behavior, see Stephen Happel, "The Bent World: Sacrament as Orthopraxis," *CTSA Proceedings* 35(1980) pp. 88-101.

that extent they will be present or lacking in their sacramental celebrations. And what holds true for the group also holds true for individuals and subgroups. For instance, sometimes individuals can be alienated from what everyone else is experiencing, or sometimes small groups at a parish Mass can be celebrating a shared life that others have no sense of. So just as the psychological effects of the sacraments are not automatic but vary with the degree of our conscious self-involvement in the ritual, so also these social effects of the sacraments are not automatic but vary according to the degree of our commitment both to what the sacraments symbolize and to those with whom we share that commitment.[35]

The second major category of the sociological effects of ritual is transition. Primarily the transition here is social, that is, a change from one set of social relationships to another; but secondarily it is also psychological, that is, a change in the way people perceive themselves in relation to God, themselves and others. In many religions there are various "rites of passage" through which individuals pass from one social status or role to another: puberty rites effecting their transition from childhood to adulthood; initiation rites making them members of special groups within the society, such as leaders, food providers, healers or diviners; wedding rites which make them married and give them an extended family of relatives. Invariably rituals of this sort have three basic phases to them: separation from one's previous status or group, suspension in a marginal state or liminal condition, and incorporation into one's new status or group.[36] Typically, symbolic gestures signal what is happening during each phase of the ritual: first, individuals are

---

[35]On this point in reference to the liturgy, see Joseph M. Powers, S.J., *Eucharistic Theology* (New York: Herder and Herder, 1967) pp. 15-18, 24-26, 73-74. With regard to the sacraments in general, see Regis A. Duffy, O.F.M., *Real Presence* (San Francisco: Harper and Row, 1982).

[36]See Wallace, pp. 127-130. This analysis of transition rituals has been generally accepted since it was first introduced in 1908 by Arnold van Gennep in *The Rites of Passage* (Chicago: University of Chicago Press, 1960).

physically removed from their previous social environment, and/or signs of their status within it are removed or covered over; secondly, the candidates are taken to a place apart, and/or they undergo a testing or are given special instructions which prepare them for their new role, and/or they are ritually processed into persons with a new status; and thirdly, they are received into their new social environment, and/or they are given signs of their new status, and/or their new role is recognized and approved by the larger group.

Many of the Catholic sacraments exhibit this same triple structure. Both the ancient and the recently revised rites for the initiation of adults take it for granted, but it is most vivid in its ancient form. In early Christian initiation people were removed from their ordinary environment for a day of fasting and prayer, after which they were stripped naked (women and men separately, to be sure) as they symbolically divested themselves of their old life. Then the candidates were immersed in water three times while three times they assented to the truths of their new faith. Finally the initiates were dried, anointed, given clean white robes, and received by the bishop and the community in their first complete celebration of the Eucharist.[37] Likewise, public penance during the patristic period was in many ways an elaborate re-entry ritual for those who by their sinfulness had withdrawn from the Christian community, and the transition or liminal period sometimes lasted for months or even years.[38]

Marriage and holy orders are obviously transition rituals bringing about new roles in the Christian community, and even a cursory examination of their rites reveals that those who are the subjects of these sacraments pass through the three symbolic phases mentioned above.

Christianity has no puberty rites as such, but since the Middle Ages three sacraments have been used to mark the transition to adult responsibility in the Church. Clearly

---

[37]See Arthur McCormack, *Christian Initiation* (New York: Hawthorn Books, 1969) pp. 43-70.

[38]See in this series, Monika Hellwig, *Sign of Reconciliation and Conversion* (Wilmington, Delaware: Michael Glazier, 1982) ch. 2.

confirmation was and still is for many a sign of spiritual strengthening and an occasion for a more mature commitment to Christ and the Church. But the first reception of penance and Eucharist have likewise been culturally celebrated as transition rituals marking children's entry into the ranks of those who can understand their religion and behave according to its norms.

In the not too distant days when people went to confession mainly to get readmitted to communion, and when the confessional was a dark box symbolically well suited to a state of liminality, penance was more visibly a rite of passage for it was an external symbol of an internal repentance or conversion. Today, however, the confessional is just as likely to be an ordinary room, and there is often less a sense of rejoining the community as there is a sense of reaffirming one's need to be reconciled with those who are in it. Yet even here there is a sense of liminality during confession and an awareness of having passed through a change of heart, if not a change in social status.

Similarly, when anointing of the sick was regarded as extreme unction for the dying, it was in many respects a transition ritual. The last rites, which include confession and communion as well as anointing, together formed a rite of passage from this life to the next, or at least they marked a change in a person's status from being ready to return to the world to being prepared to go to heaven. This passage aspect is less apparent in the new ritual for anointing, although it can still be administered to the dying, and sometimes it marks a change in a person's status from being seriously sick to being on the road to recovery. Moreover, as James Empereur points out, illness itself is a liminal state, removed from the rhythms of ordinary life, and in need of interpretation. "Anointing is the liturgy which clarifies that suffering and sickness are not symbols of sin but of grace, not of testing and purification, but of a more intimate relationship with God."[39] Communal celebrations of this

---

[39] James Empereur, S.J., *Prophetic Anointing* (Wilmington, Delaware: Michael Glazier, 1982) p. 154.

sacrament can also affect the relation between the sick and well in a parish, bringing about more caring relationships as those who attend them learn who may need their help and why they deserve to receive it.

Some of the social effects of transition rituals occur quite readily, almost mechanically, while others do not. Those which occur most readily are those which are changes in social roles in the Church. A person who is baptized, for example, is immediately and irrevocably a member of the Church. Likewise, someone who is ordained automatically receives a role within the ecclesiastical community, and someone who is married receives a status which can be lost only by the death of the spouse. The immediacy and permanence of these effects were historically factors in the development of the theological concept of the sacramental character, an indelible sign on the souls of individuals who were baptized or ordained, as well as in the development of the concept of the marriage bond, which was sometimes likened to a sacramental character.[40]

There is another group of social effects, however, which do not occur quite so automatically. Hopefully, those who are baptized will live up to their calling as Christians, those who are ordained will be good priests, and those who are married will be faithful spouses. The change in one's social role makes it possible to carry out that role well (only those who are ordained can possibly be holy priests, for instance) but it does not make it necessary. Again historically, this aspect of sacramental effectiveness seems to have been reflected in the way that theology spoke of the further effects of these sacraments as grace, or sacramental graces. As it was traditionally understood, sacramental grace was always offered to those who received a sacrament, but its actual effectiveness in their soul depended on their willingness to cooperate with it.

Now, lest it appear that the theological dimensions of the sacraments can be reduced to their sociological and psycho-

---

[40]See Leeming, p. 368.

logical dimensions, it must be pointed out that some sacramental effects can be studied by the empirical human sciences while others cannot. Changes that a sacrament brings about in an individual's relationship with God, for instance, cannot be observed or explained by sociologists and psychologists. Such scientists can only discuss changes in social relationships and changes in individual behavior and awareness. But these changes can also be understood as having theological ramifications, and so theologians can talk about them in their own ways, ways which are not available to the secular sciences. The medieval adage was that "grace builds on nature," and here it can be taken to indicate that the realm of the properly human (that is, the order of nature) is presupposed and subsumed into the realm of grace or God's free gift (that is, the supernatural order). In a parallel fashion, systematic theology builds on the empirical human sciences, for it accepts their verified conclusions but then goes beyond them to discuss things like conversion and prayer, the Church and the sacraments, in its own unique manner. In the present work, for example, the properly theological aspects of the sacraments are not directly addressed until Part Two, although they are brought in by way of illustration and discussed as historical examples (even in Chapter IV) here in Part One.

Let us go on, then, to the third major category of the sociological effects of rituals, which is communication. Just as everyday rituals communicate the beliefs and values, attitudes and behaviors of an older generation to a younger generation, so also religious rituals communicate specifically religious ideas and ideals, affective orientations and patterns of living to a younger generation of believers.[41] Religious ritual can be said to symbolically articulate the shared religious experience of a community by putting into words and getures what it understands about itself, about individuals, and about the relation of both to the transcendent. In doing so it transmits both that experience and that

[41]On ritual as communication, see Wallace, pp. 233-243; also Mary Douglas, *Natural Symbols* (New York: Vintage Books, 1973) ch. 3.

understanding through history, and it effects its perdurance into the future. Before the gospels were written the first Christians continued as a church and passed on the revelation they had received in Jesus largely through their liturgical celebrations. Similarly, the Jews survived as a people and Judaism survived as a religion through the centuries of diaspora mainly by means of home-centered rituals such as the yearly Passover supper and the daily recitation of the psalms. And in our own century Catholics were not only legally bound to attend Sunday Mass but they were also counselled that "the family that prays together stays together." Both the law and the counsel had the effect of maintaining a religious identity and passing it on to the upcoming generation.[42]

But young people are not the only ones in need of what can be communicated through ritual. Human memory fails; human will falters. As Monika Hellwig often reminds us, the root meaning of *anamnesis* (the ancient Greek word for what happens in liturgy) is not "remembering" but "not forgetting." We all need to be regularly reminded of who we are and what we are called to be, lest we forget. And if we are growing in our understanding and appreciation of the Christian life we need to receive direction for that growth from our religious community. Although they cannot do it all, the rituals of the liturgy and the sacraments can provide at least some of that direction. Ritual is therefore one of the places in which adult believers allow the depth and richness of their religious tradition to be communicated to them. It is also a place where they can communicate it to themselves, so to speak, by the words that they speak and the actions that they perform. Finally it is a place where they can publicly profess their faith to other adults by joining in ceremonial enactments of their central beliefs.[43]

In the words of Edward Fischer, "All ritual is communication. As communication, ritual speaks to our minds, and

---

[42] See Kavanagh in *The Roots of Ritual*, pp. 148-154.

[43] See John E. Smith, *Experience and God* (New York: Oxford University Press, 1968) p. 58.

spirits, and intuitions by means of words, sights, sounds, and smells."[44] Fischer's point as an expert in communication arts, however, is that "communication is effective only if it fits the times. Communication is blurred when one attempts to use forms that are no longer fitting."[45] As we noted in the first chapter, symbols can die, they can become empty signs. This can happen because of individual and psychological reasons when they no longer express the conscious religious experience of those who use the symbols, but it can also happen because of cultural or social reasons when people no longer perceive what they have experienced as holy through the symbols that they are given by their tradition. The history of the Catholic sacraments themselves bears adequate testimony to this. In their external forms they have sometimes changed markedly during a transition from one cultural epoch to another: periodically the symbols were altered to fit the new social situations in which the Church found itself.[46]

Some of the disparity between what sacramental symbols are meant to communicate and what they actually do communicate can, no doubt, be reduced through education. As Monika Hellwig suggests, "We have in the sacraments a whole language of gestures, signs, symbols, stories, allusions, and we have long ago forgotten the vocabulary and grammar of the language. To understand what is being expressed, we have to try to remember the language."[47] On the other hand, Edward Fischer urges that education cannot be the whole answer: "To try to formulate a ritual meaningful to all people at all times is a form of pride that anyone interested in communication cannot afford."[48] In other words, for the sacraments to be effective communicators of

---

[44]Edward Fischer, "Ritual as Communication," in *The Roots of Ritual*, p. 161.

[45]Same, p. 165.

[46]See Joseph Martos, *Doors to the Sacred* (New York: Doubleday, 1981) chs. 6-12.

[47]Monika Hellwig, *The Meaning of the Sacraments* (Dayton, Ohio: Pflaum /Standard, 1972) p. 3.

[48]Fischer in *Roots of Ritual*, p. 165.

what they symbolize, people must not only learn the language of the symbols, but the symbols must also speak the language of the people. There must be adaptation on both sides of the liturgical equation. Of course there is always a danger that adjusting symbolic rituals to the mentality of those who participate in them can lead to a loss of their original meaning, but not adjusting them is a fairly certain way of lessening their ability to communicate that meaning. "If we try to make one ritual for everyone from eight to eighty, learned and unlearned, civilized and semi-barbaric, we are out of touch with reality."[49]

In this section we have looked at religious rituals as agents of unification, transition and communication. Although it may be that some rituals have all three effects, not all rituals must have all of them. In the past, the emergency baptism of infants, private confession and the individualized administration of extreme unction may have had few if any socially unifying effects. In the present, most celebrations of the Eucharist and some celebrations of reconciliation and anointing are not socially transition rituals even though they may effect individual treansitions along the order of conversion or reconversion. And although all rituals usually communicate something at least, in both the past and the present the effectiveness of sacramental communication has often been less than it could be.

4. The Historical Dimension

It is by no means obvious that religion has a history. We may be familiar with the changes in the Catholic Church during recent decades, and we may even know something about the history of Christianity. Few Catholics suspect, however, that the past two or three millennia may be part of a larger stretch of religious history. Instead, we tend to view African religions, the Greek and Roman gods, Judaism,

---

[49]Same, p. 166.

Protestantism, and other religions simply as "different" from our own. We also tend to judge that they are "not the true religion," although we grant that some are closer to us (and therefore closer to the truth) than others.

To sociologists, this is a subjective and ethnocentric view of religion. In fact, every ethnic or cultural group tends at first to judge that its ways are "right" and that the ways of others are good or bad depending on how closely they approximate the "right" ways of believing or behaving. The scientific study of religion, on the other hand, tries not to favor any one religion by judging others against its standards. Instead, it tries to objectively understand each religion on its own merits, and to understand how it is related to other religions.

When religions are thus lined up side by side, so to speak, similarities between certain ones seem to suggest religious groupings or style sets. The native religions of Africa, North and South America, and Australia seem to naturally fall into one set. Traditional Judaism, Christianity and Islam fall easily into a strongly monotheistic group. There are still other ways of grouping religions, and when these groups are placed on a historical time line they suggest a pattern of evolution or sequential development in the complex cultural phenomenon known generally as religion.

Robert Bellah has proposed that there are five stages in the evolution of the world's religions,[50] but for our purposes we may group them into just three main phases or cultural styles.[51] These correspond to the three main stages in the evolution of human cultures, the first being the period of tribal culture extending from the origins of the human race to somewhere around 5000 BC, the second being the period of civilized culture extending from the invention of farming

---

[50]See Robert N. Bellah, "Religious Evolution," *American Sociological Review* 29(1964) pp. 358-374, collected in *Beyond Belief* (New York: Harper and Row, 1970) pp. 20-50. Also using this paradigm is Barbara Hargrove in the work cited above, chs. 5-7.

[51]See Nottingham, ch. 2; also, Kenneth Boulding, *The Meaning of the Twentieth Century: The Great Transition* (New York: Harper and Row, 1964) pp. 1-16.

and the discovery of metal to the development of modern science, and the third being a new and as yet unnamed cultural style which began about 1500 AD in Europe and which is still emerging and spreading around the globe. The three main phases of religion which correspond to these cultural epochs may be conveniently called primitive, classical and modern.[52]

Primitive religion is so called not because it is crude or simple (it may be incredibly complex) but because it is the first (*primus* in Latin) and most basic form of human religiosity. It thus dates from prehistoric times but it is also found among tribal peoples today. Certain aspects of primitive religion are also considered basic to all religion, for example, the experience of the sacred, concern for understanding the mysteries of life and the cosmos, and the expression of religious meaning in myth and ritual. Its main features may be quickly summarized:

> Primitive religion is based on a near fusion of the religion and the rest of life. The individual performs certain religious acts because of the role he or she plays in the group. Primitive religion is not concerned with a clearly defined mythology or theology; instead it is an expression of values, desires and emotions. It makes little use of specialized functionaries, with the exception of the shaman, who tends to provide in his or her person a center for the emotional content of crisis occasions. It is in such crisis situations that primitive religion is expected to operate, whether they be the crises of individual life — birth, death, changes of status — or those of the group — war, the cycles of production, problems of order. Primitive religion serves to bind the society together in affirmation of common purpose, giving individuals the sense of participating in such purpose and finding identity in it.[53]

---

[52] Bellah's name for his five stages are primitive, archaic, historic, early modern, and modern. He admits, however, that the fourth is something like a transitional stage; I would contend that the same is true of the second stage.

[53] Hargrove, p. 80.

In other words, early human culture is relatively undifferentiated. Societies are the size of families, clans or tribes at the largest, and although individuals in these groups have assignable roles, the societies themselves are fairly homogeneous. The hand-to-mouth existence of small hunting and gathering societies is no place for economic stratification and extended social ranking; the predominant social reality is what Turner calls *communitas*. Although local control is largely authoritarian, the main social controls are embodied not in individuals but in customs and traditions to which even the tribal leaders must submit. So on the one hand there is little room for individualism and innovation, but on the other hand there is great social stability which allows for the passing on of accumulated wisdom from one generation to the next across tens of thousands of years.

Similarly, primitive human consciousness is relatively undifferentiated. There is no distinction between objective and subjective truth: what is so, is so; and what is not so, is not so. But "truth" here is primarily practical: it is the truth of how to be a good child or husband or wife, of how to hunt or fish, of how to build a canoe or a house, of how to integrate oneself into the cycle of seasons and the stages of life. The emphasis is therefore on orthopraxis (right action) rather than on orthodoxy (right belief), and to a great extent all mythic embodiments of a practical truth (even seemingly contradictory stories) are equally true. Because these practical truths are also sacred truths, the natural is not distinguished from the supernatural, and the holy is experienced as something within the world. Moreover, *my* world is the same as *our* world, and *our* world is the same as *the* world, for when widely scattered tribal groups are separated from each other by distance and language there is little awareness that other people can think and behave differently. Primitive consciousness is thus a holistic awareness of oneself as fitting within the pattern of existence which is portrayed in the lifestyle and myths of one's society.

Finally, primitive religion is likewise holistic, covering all areas of individual and social life. Its myths portray paradigms of human action and paragons of human virtue, and its rituals give people a way of entering into these and acting them out. "In the ritual the participants become identified with the mythical beings they represent. The mythical beings are not addressed or propitiated or beseeched. The distance between man and mythical being, which was at best slight, disappears altogether in the moment of ritual when everywhen becomes now. There are no priests and no congregation, no mediating representative roles and no spectators. All present are involved in the ritual action itself and have become one with the myth."[54]

Such was the universal state of human culture and religion for untold millennia. Then, beginning around seven thousand years ago, a few basic discoveries and inventions initiated a gradual transformation of some societies primarily in the Middle and Far East. The discovery that seeds could be collected and planted, that animals could be raised for slaughter or domesticated for labor, made it both possible and desirable for large numbers of people to live relatively close to one another. Agriculture thus encouraged the rise of towns and then cities, and with cities began the style of social organization known as civilization (*civis* in Latin means "city"). The invention of writing to keep track of produce and business transactions later led to the rise of literature including religious scriptures. The discovery that ores could be smelted into metals led to improvements in tools for farming and weapons for war.

Whenever it occurs, the rise of civilization brings with it a division of labor (into rulers, farmers, artisans, merchants, scribes, soldiers) and a stratification of society (into citizens and slaves, literate and illiterate, wealthy and poor). Spontaneous communitas is gone and in its place come social distinctions which alienate individuals and groups from one another. This differentiation of society is also found in religion. Religious institutions (temple, church, religious ritual) begin to be separated from other social institutions (government, family, civic

---

[54]Bellah, *Beyond Belief*, p. 28. For more on primitive religious ritual, see Wallace, pp. 216-233.

ritual); religious functionaries (priests, scholars, administrators) begin to emerge as a separate class (sacred caste, clergy); and in many instances religion too is divided between the way of perfection open only to a few (saints and prophets, monks and nuns) and the way of salvation available to the many.

It can even be said that the hallmark of classical religion, both non-Christian and Christian, is the desire for salvation. Classical religion introduces the practice of sacrifice which despite its many forms (vegetable, animal, human) is also an attempt to establish, maintain or restore a good relationship with the divine. The aim of all sacrifice is therefore unity: either unity with a divinity in spiritual communion (and most sacrifices had ritual meals connected with them) or unity with the divine will (doing what should be done during the religious ritual and in the rest of life). But sacrifice is not the only way that salvation may be sought in classical religions; at one time or another, in one place or another, people have tried to achieve salvation through actions (obeying commandments, performing rituals), knowledge (mystical intuition, rational reflection) and devotion (dedication, fervor).[55]

Moreover, of these three elements (action, knowledge and devotion), it is the cognitive which is emphasized during religion's classical phase. Belief is distinguished from practice, and faith is contrasted with works, but priority is regularly given to ideas rather than deeds. Classical religions therefore tend to insist on orthodoxy rather than orthopraxis, allowing diversity in practice whenever it can be reconciled with uniformity in doctrine. Compared with the indifference that comes of ignorance about others during its primitive phase, religion in its classical phase recognizes differences and is generally intolerant of them. Only one religion can be the true religion and so other beliefs must be either heretical (if the differences are minor) or simply erroneous (if the differences are major). Most classical religions have therefore been expansionist in one way or another (for example, the Greek pantheon displaced the

---

[55] See J. Milton Yinger, *Religion, Society and the Individual* (New York: Macmillan, 1957) p. 88. On various aspects and types of salvation, see pp. 85-90.

Egyptian gods after the conquest by Alexander the Great; Buddhism and Confucianism have been spread by disciples; Christianity and Islam have supported both holy wars and missionary efforts) and they have provided both for the conversion of others to the true faith and for the reconciliation of those who wander from the fold.

Clearly, then, classical religious consciousness includes strong elements of differentiation. Typically the divine is strongly distinguished from the human, the supernatural from the natural, and religion is largely conceived as an attempt to overcome man's estrangement from God or the gods. Even the picturing of the divinity as one or many, and the depicting of his (or her or their) attributes, mirror to some extent the vertical and lateral distinctions that are found in society.[56] Cultic worship or praying to the gods "up there" is a classical religious practice, and even the word "religion," coined in ancient Rome, meant to "to bind back" or "to reunite." This reunion with the divine, furthermore, is often to be accomplished by a rejection of this world and its values, either physically (asceticism, monasticism) or psychically (meditation, contemplation). Sometimes this is also accompanied by a prophetic judgment that the present social order does not meet divinely revealed standards. In other words, classical religious consciousness is able to perceive a discrepancy between the way things are and the way things ought to be, and the distinction between the sacred and the profane makes it possible for religious leaders to criticize the sinfulness of secular society.[57]

Almost all of the world's "great" religions — Hinduism, Buddhism, Confucianism, Judaism, Christianity, Islam — began during the classical phase of religion. With the exception of Hinduism (which evolved slowly out of the tribal religions of India) all of them are traceable to unique individuals — Buddha, Confucius, Moses, Jesus, Mohammed — whose religious experience and insight made a break with

---

[56] See Guy E. Swanson, *The Birth of the Gods* (Ann Arbor: University of Michigan Press, 1960) esp. pp. 55-81.

[57] See Bellah, same, p. 35f.

the past and provided a foundation for a new religious tradition. They were charismatic persons in Max Weber's sense of the term, and so the religions that they initiated are to a greater or lesser extent institutionalizations of their charismatic personality. Their words are enshrined in religious scriptures, their actions become models for religious practices, their leadership is passed on first to disciples and then to religious authorities. This "routinization of charisma" makes it possible for later generations of believers to follow in their founder's footsteps; but it is also possible for non-charismatic concerns and behavior to slip into the tradition and get routinized in religious institutions that bear little resemblance to the founder's ideas or ideals.[58]

It was partly in reaction to what they perceived as departures from Christ's gospel that the sixteenth century reformers (especially Martin Luther and John Calvin) protested against the institutions of medieval Christianity. But the religious perception of the Protestants was also sharpened by the cultural shift which was beginning during the Renaissance. The invention of the printing press made books more affordable, and books made it possible to read about the world from many points of view and to develop one's own perspective on matters. European explorers found civilizations in Asia and the Americas, calling into question the classical assumption that the human race could be neatly divided into the civilized and non-civilized world. Astronomers and other scientists demonstrated that the earth was neither flat nor the center of the universe, making it possible to doubt many of the traditional conceptions of reality. Emerging nationalism was also weakening the medieval ideal of a single Christian society and at the same time it was strengthening the notion that political pluralism was desirable.[59] In other words, the Renaissance marked the

[58] See Max Weber, *On Charisma and Institution Building* (Chicago: University of Chicago Press, 1968) pp. 48-65, 253-283. For a summary treatment, see O'Dea, p. 37f.

[59] For a sense of how the modern world has been restructuring human perception, read Marshall McLuhan, *The Gutenberg Galaxy* (Toronto: University of Toronto Press, 1962), and *Understanding Media* (New York: McGraw Hill, 1964).

beginning of the end of classical culture and the beginning of the modern epoch. And the Protestant Reformation which occurred during the Renaissance was therefore both a religious protest against the routinization of corruption in the Church and a modern protest against medieval ways of institutionalizing the Christian message in hierarchy, dogma and sacrament.

At its beginning and even through the twentieth century Protestantism has borne many resemblences to traditional Catholicism (for example, insistence on dogma, intolerance of diversity, emphasis on salvation). But early Protestantism also displayed certain elements of religion which were to become distinctive marks of the third phase of religious evolution.

> The defining characteristic of modern religion is the collapse of hierarchical structuring of both this and the other world. The dualism of the historic religions remains as a feature of early modern religion but takes on a new significance in the context of more direct confrontation between the two worlds. Under the new circumstances salvation is not to be found in any kind of withdrawal from the world but in the midst of worldly activities.... What the Reformation did was in principle, with the usual reservations and mortgages to the past, break through the whole mediated system of salvation and declare salvation potentially available to any man no matter what his state or calling might be.[60]

It is hard for Catholics today to appreciate the radical break with the past that Protestantism initiated, since most of us share many of the same cultural religious assumptions that the Reformation was based on. Conservative Catholics sometimes complain that the Church is becoming more Protestant, but from a sociological perspective it is more

---

[60] Bellah, same, p. 36.

correct to say that Catholicism since Vatican II is allowing itself to enter into the cultural transformation which is slowly changing the shape of human society all over the globe. Electric communication and rapid transportation pull people out of their regional isolation and force them to respect the reality of pluralism. The extended family which stayed down on the farm is being replaced by the nuclear family which moves to where the jobs are, and the stability of marriage is being overtaken by the statistical regularity of divorce. The old colonial empires have been broken up, while corporations are decentralizing and companies are diversifying. National boundaries are blurred by international trade agreements and intercontinental political treaties, as well as by multinational corporations and regional cartels. As social mobility increases, society becomes less stratified by distinct classes. As education increases, people are less willing to accept any authority as absolute. As the rate of change increases, change itself gets taken for granted, not only in society at large but also in religious institutions.[61]

Modern consciousness reflects this revolution in modern culture. At least in technologically advanced countries which are experiencing the full effects of these changes, and in those segments of society where the change is actually occurring, people live not in one world but in many: home, business, civic, church, school, friends, recreation, and so on. As a result, consciousness becomes highly differentiated, with the greatest differentiation generally occurring in the most educated: not only is the realm of the sacred distinguished from the profane realm, but common sense practicality is distinguished from scholarly research, scientific theorizing is distinguished from technological application, and artistic creativity is distinguished from philosophical reflection. People get used to looking at things from different angles, and they recognize that others

---

[61] For a wide-ranging assessment of the global restructuring of society, see Alvin Toffler, *The Third Wave* (New York: William Morrow, 1980).

bring to any situation their own perspective or unique cluster of perspectives. Consequently, they have a greater respect for differences and a greater tolerance of pluralism. Although they may select a career or join an interest group or push for a certain cause, they are also aware (or at least they suspect) that their position represents values which they themselves have chosen and which they are responsible for actualizing.

At the same time that modern consciousness becomes so highly differentiated, however, it also becomes highly integrative. There is a growing sense that specialization is not the last word either in human knowledge or in personal development. There is an awareness that somehow everything is connected with everything else, and that things must be seen in relation to other things and to some sort of whole. World economists and international diplomats speak of interdependence among nations. Ecologists insist that businessmen and politicians reckon with the impact of their decisions on the natural environment, while sociologists do the same with respect to the human environment. Educators discover the value implications of their "value-free" disciplines, and physicians are confronted with the ethical implications of their medical practices. In religion too, the awareness of diversity leads not only to a respect for religious differences but also to an ecumenical desire for religious unity, or at least to a desire to discover a commonality that underlies diverse religious traditions.

Thus modern religious consciousness is at once both differentiated and integrative. It acknowledges and respects religious diversity but it also supposes that similarities in religious ideals and values are ultimately more important than differences in doctrine or ritual. It recognizes that religious doctrines are distinct from religious experiences and yet at the same time it insists that doctrines should be relevant to people's lives. In this sense modern religious consciousness calls for a reunification of theory and practice in a theology that has practical implications. Such consciousness also recognizes a need for holiness but, to borrow

Josef Goldbrunner's phrase, it assumes that "holiness is wholeness" and not a separate sphere of development. And it is more concerned with individual authenticity based on personal conversion and commitment than it is with intellectual adherence to beliefs which may or may not correspond to the way one behaves.

In many ways the "central feature" of modern religion is "the collapse of the dualism that was so crucial to all the historic religions."[62] Not long ago it was important to distinguish sharply between the natural and the supernatural, the human and the divine, truth and error, clergy and laity, Christians and non-Christians, and so on. Today, however, it seems more appropriate to speak of grace within the world, the divine incarnate in the human, the perspectival nature of knowledge, the ministry of the laity, and even anonymous Christians. Nevertheless, this rejection of classical religious dualism "is not to be interpreted as a return to primitive monism: it is not that a single world has replaced a double one but that an infinitely multiplex one has replaced the simple duplex structure."[63] On the one hand this means that modern consciousness accepts the different perspectives from which religion can be viewed (psychology, sociology, history, philosophy, political science, etc.) and it is not afraid that the unity or uniqueness of religion will thereby be lost. On the other hand this means that modern religion accepts diversity both within the totality of world religions and within the confines of a single religious tradition. Modern Catholics freely admit, for example, that there have been vast differences in their sacramental practices over the course of twenty centuries, and they are beginning to acknowledge the admissibility of simultaneous diversity in the sacramental practices in the variety of Catholic cultures around the world.

At the same time, however, the modern acceptance of

---

[62] Bellah, same, p. 40.
[63] Same.

pluralism poses a unique problem with respect to religious symbolism. In the words of Mary Douglas, "One of the gravest problems of our day is the lack of commitment to common symbols."[64] As Douglas in her own way shows, one of the greatest unifying factors of traditional Christianity was the presence of "condensed symbols," both creedal statements and ritual practices which everyone acknowledged as essential to their faith and representative of their commitment.[65] But today, in Christianity as a whole there appear to be few if any symbolic statements or actions which "say a lot" to all Christians the world over. Elizabeth Nottingham expresses this even more emphatically:

> In fact, no single universally accepted system of religious symbolism exists. Insofar as the various religious organizations are able to commend their officially sanctioned symbol systems to their membership, a plurality of symbol systems may be said to coexist simultaneously. Furthermore, many individuals, even organizational members, feel at liberty to interpret freely — or even repudiate — traditional symbol systems handed down by hierarchical or other religious authority.[66]

But the source of this inability to accept a single symbol system is not an individual or even a cultural rejection of symbolism as such. Rather it is the other way around. The modern desire for integration leads to a rejection of symbols which are felt to be empty or powerless, even if they were traditionally rich and potent symbols, and to an insistence on symbols which authentically express and communicate religious experience and understanding. Furthermore, there is "a growing awareness among the religiously affiliated and nonaffiliated alike that symbols *are* symbols and that man in the last analysis is responsible for the choice of his symbolism."[67] In other words, the modern differentiation between

[64]Douglas, p. 19.
[65]Same, ch. 3.
[66]Nottingham, p. 41.
[67]Same, p. 42; see also Bellah, same, p. 42.

the symbolic and the real at the same time reveals the responsibility that people have for making their symbolic statements — and sacraments are symbolic statements — truly representative of religious realities.[68]

One conclusion which can be drawn from this brief overview of religious evolution is that if Catholicism today is to be practiced and lived in tribal, agricultural and industrial societies (for Catholicism finds itself among peoples with each of these predominant cultural patterns), then the style of its sacraments may be expected to vary greatly once the Church appreciates the sociological implications of its long allegiance to the classical style of religion (and to the correspondingly traditional style of theology). At the same time, however, an awareness of how religion and religious symbolism function in any type of culture should make it easier to develop authentic sacramental forms for each of them.

A second conclusion is that if religion is currently undergoing a transition as momentous as the change from primitive to civilized society, then the cultural style of sacraments in technologically advanced societies cannot be expected to remain what it was during the classical period of Christianity. This does not imply, however, that modern religion or sacramental practice in the future will be totally different from what they were in the past. As Erik Erikson and other developmental psychologists insist, wherever true development takes place the accomplishments of earlier stages are retained and subsumed within later stages of growth. Modern religion, therefore, if it is truly modern and truly religious, will contain primitive elements such as the experience of the sacred and its articulation in myth and ritual, but it will also contain classical elements such as concern for conceptual clarity and the ability to prophetically contrast transcendent ideals with actual realities. Likewise, modern Catholic ritual will not reject the seven traditional sacraments but rather it will retain many of the elements in them and subsume these within a new sacramental style.

[68]On the need for authenticity in sacramental action, see Regis Duffy, cited in n. 35 above.

Recommended Reading

Barbara Hargrove, *The Sociology of Religion: Classical and Contemporary Approaches* (Arlington Heights, Illinois: AHM Publishing Corporation, 1979) is a thorough but very readable introduction to the subject, with background on ritual and sacraments in Parts I and II.

Thomas F. O'Dea, *The Sociology of Religion* (Englewood Cliffs, New Jersey: Prentice Hall, 1966) contains clear and summary treatments of many of the concepts discussed in this chapter.

Elizabeth K. Nottingham, *Religion: A Sociological View* (New York: Random House, 1971) is a broad introductory survey to the field which gives a three-stage account of cultural and religious evolution.

Louis Schneider, *Sociological Approach to Religion* (New York: John Wiley and Sons, 1970) has a long chapter on the structural functional analysis of religion.

Anthony F. C. Wallace, *Religion: An Anthropological View* (New York: Random House, 1966) gives special attention to the function of ritual in primitive religions.

Gregory Baum, *Religion and Alienation: A Theological Reading of Sociology* (New York: Paulist Press, 1975) sees classical and contemporary sociology as discovering many of the same basic human realities that are discussed in Christian theology.

Peter Berger, *The Sacred Canopy: Elements of a Sociological Theory of Religion* (New York: Doubleday, 1967) discusses the traditionally strong and recently declining role of religion in constructing the social world. However, *A Rumor of Angels: Modern Society and the Rediscovery of the Supernatural* (New York: Doubleday, 1969) suggests that despite modern secularization there are still signs of transcendence that point to a further dimension of reality.

James Shaughnessy, ed., *The Roots of Ritual* (Grand Rapids, Michigan: William B. Eerdmans, 1971) is a collection of articles primarily on the social and cultural dimensions of ritual.

CHAPTER III: HISTORY AND THE SACRAMENTS

The sacraments did not fall from heaven, fully formed. They have a history through which they took shape and got reshaped by successive generations of Catholic practice, canonical regulation and theological interpretation. As rituals they went through periods of development and even decline. As occasions for religious experience they have been affected by the psychological dispositions of those who participated in them. As events in the religious life of a believing community they have been altered by the social style of the cultures through which they were handed down. And like the sacraments themselves, sacramental theology has also undergone changes in both form and content during the Christian centuries.

1. Historical Investigation into the Sacraments

In response to the Protestant Reformation, the Council of Trent called for a Catholic counter-reformation, a major focus of which was the Mass and the sacraments. To refute the reformers' allegations that ecclesiastical worship was a non-biblical, medieval invention, church historians and liturgical scholars began the first comprehensive search through archives and libraries for evidence which linked the sixteenth century liturgy to its patristic and apostolic beginnings. What they found was far from complete, but it was enough to demonstrate that the major elements in Catholic worship were indeed quite ancient, and it was enough to give liturgists a sound basis on which to develop the missal and sacramentary which the Church then used for the better part of four centuries.[1]

Despite the liturgical stability which came out of these reforms, historical inquiry into the ancient and medieval periods of Christian worship continued in the seventeenth and eighteenth centuries, but for the most part the fruits of that research were known only to scholars with antiquarian interests. Theologians and canonists made little use of these findings in trying to understand the sacraments and in deciding how they were to be properly performed. The general Catholic consensus seemed to be that the sacramental system had reached its apex, and so further change was unnecessary.

In the nineteenth century, however, Prosper Gueranger founded the monastery of Solesmes in France and through his inspiration the Benedictines in Europe sparked a renewed interest in Christian worship and Gregorian chant. Their major concern, however, was not antiquarian but pastoral, to reawaken people's appreciation for the liturgical life of the Church. It was the beginning of what today we call the modern liturgical movement. But though their interests were ultimately pastoral, their initial efforts were largely historical, for they believed that a sound liturgical piety could only be based on a solid foundation of liturgical scholarship.

Even before the First World War, a great deal of historical foundation laying had been accomplished: texts of the *Didache* (second century), *The Apostolic Tradition* (third

---

[1] For a more complete history of liturgical studies, see William J. O'Shea, "Liturgiology," *New Catholic Encyclopedia* (New York: McGraw Hill, 1966) Vol. VIII, pp. 919-927. For a review of recent studies and their impact on theology, see Albert Houssian, "La redécouverte de la liturgie par la théologie sacramentaire (1950-1980)," *La Maison-Dieu* 149(1982) pp. 27-55.

century), the *Anaphora of St. Serapion*, (fourth century), and *The Apostolic Constitutions* (fifth century), as well as other ancient liturgical documents were discovered (or rediscovered) and published; new editions of the Gelasian, Gregorian and Leonine sacramentaries (Roman, fifth and sixth centuries) as well as Eastern rite liturgies (Greek, Armenian, Syrian) were issued; voluminous collections of ancient and medieval texts were begun; academic encyclopedias systematized what was being discovered; scholarly journals were founded in France, Belgium, Holland and Germany to publish the results of liturgical research. Some of the books of that period which attempted to summarize the history of the liturgy on the basis of what was then becoming known have remained classics in the field.[2]

On this solid and expanding base of historical documentation, scholars during the period between the two great European wars began to reconstruct the history of Christian worship in all its aspects: the Mass and the sacraments, the liturgical year, the liturgy of the hours (the divine office), monastic and religious music and art, liturgical vestments and sacred vessels. Slowly but surely the edifice began to take shape, now under the leadership of Lambert Beauduin at the monastery of Mont-César in Belgium and Ildefons Herwegen at the abbey of Maria Laach in Germany. The results of these historical and liturgical investigations continued to be published in scholarly journals, but in addition, the less technical and more pastoral aspects of these studies began to be made more widely available through periodicals generally read by seminary and college teachers, bishops and priests.

It was not until after the Second World War that the work begun almost a century before began to take final form. At last it was possible to see how all the elements of the

[2]Louis Duchesne, *Christian Worship: Its Origins and Evolution* (Eng. trans. London: SPCK, 1902); Edmund Bishop, *Liturgica Historica* (Oxford: Clarendon Press, 1918) collects articles written earlier; Ludwig Eisenhofer and Joseph Lechner, *The Liturgy of the Roman Rite* (Eng. trans. New York: Herder and Herder, 1961) is based on research begun by Valentin Thalhofer in the nineteenth century.

Church's worship had come together and assumed their place in the Tridentine rites.[3] And at last it was possible to publish rather complete histories of the Mass and each of the seven sacraments. Almost simultaneously, two scholars working independently drew together decades of earlier investigations to produce thorough accounts of the history of the Eucharist.[4] Inspired by their success, similar studies of the other sacraments began to appear in Herder's *Handbuch der Dogmengeschichte*[5] and in Édition du Cerf's series, *Lex Orandi*.[6] It was not until somewhat later, however, that comprehensive historical treatments of marriage[7] and orders[8] became available.

What showed clearly through all these histories, moreover, was that the development of the Mass and the sacraments had been neither simple nor uniform, and that the Tridentine missal and sacramentary had excluded much of the variety in the Church's liturgical tradition. In their efforts to make Catholic worship more truly catholic (by recovering dimensions of public worship which had existed prior to Trent), leaders of the liturgical movement began to suggest changes which would increase people's participation in and appreciation of ecclesiastical prayer.[9] These

---

[3]See Mario Righetti, *Manuale di Storia Liturgica* (Milan: Editrice Àncora, 4 vols., 1946-49), which covered almost all aspects of church worship.

[4]Dom Gregory Dix, *The Shape of the Liturgy* (London: Dacré Press, 1946); Josef Jungmann, S.J., *The Mass of the Roman Rite* (Eng. trans. New York: Benziger, 2 vols. 1951, 1955).

[5]The first volume on the sacraments appeared in 1951. Two of these have been translated into English: Burkhard Neunheuser, O.S.B., *Baptism and Confirmation* (New York: Herder and Herder, 1964); Bernhard Poschmann, *Penance and the Anointing of the Sick* (New York: Herder and Herder, 1964).

[6]The series was begun in 1944, but few of these books have been translated into English and none of the sacramental histories.

[7]Edward Schillebeeckx, O.P., *Marriage: Human Reality and Saving Mystery* (Eng. trans. New York: Sheed and Ward, 1965); Theodore Mackin, S.J., *What is Marriage?* (New York: Paulist Press, 1982).

[8]Bernard Cooke, *Ministry to Word and Sacraments* (Philadelphia: Fortress Press, 1976).

[9]See, for example, Godfrey Diekmann, O.S.B., *Come, Let Us Worship* (Baltimore: Helicon Press, 1961).

suggestions were based on sound liturgical scholarship,[10] but they were also based on solid biblical research and recent developments in sacramental theology.[11] The movement gained additional momentum through yearly liturgical conferences in a number of countries, which brought together scholars and pastors to discuss new ideas and possibilities, as well as through periodic international meetings of liturgical experts themselves to share their discoveries about the past and hopes for the future. This momentum culminated in the liturgical reforms approved by the Second Vatican Council, but the effects of the liturgical movement are still being felt in the recent revision of the Church's code of canon law, in the growing desire for more regional autonomy in ecclesiastical worship, and in other ways.

Even from this sketch of modern liturgical research and its implications, it is clear that a full history of the sacraments cannot be presented in a single chapter of a short book.[12] What can be presented, however, in a way that provides a bridge between the sociological history of religion discussed in the previous chapter and the current theological interpretations of the sacraments to be discussed in the next chapter, is a brief history of Catholic *sacramentality*. For beneath the visible changes in the Church's sacraments over the past twenty centuries, there have been underlying changes which have shown in different phases of what might be called sacramental form or style.[13]

---

[10]See William J. O'Shea, S.S., *The Worship of the Church* (Westminster, Maryland: Newman Press, 1957); Cyprian Vaggagini, O.S.B., *Theological Dimensions of the Liturgy* (Eng. trans. Collegeville, Minnesota: Liturgical Press, 1959); Aimé Georges Martimort, *L'Église en Prière* (Tournai, Belgium: Desclee, 1961).

[11]See the next chapter.

[12]For a more complete but unannotated history of the sacraments, see Joseph Martos, *Doors to the Sacred* (New York: Doubleday, 1981).

[13]For a somewhat different but illuminating approach to changes in Christian sacramentality through seven historical periods, see Marion J. Hatchett, *Sanctifying Life, Time and Space* (New York: Seabury Press, 1976).

2. The Apostolic Period

Even secular historians must admit that Jesus of Nazareth was a charismatic individual. During his brief ministry he drew crowds of people who were sincerely interested or merely curious about him; he attracted a band of faithful followers who traveled with him and afterwards preserved the memory of what he had said and done; and he aroused enough antagonism among the religious and political leaders of Palestine that they had him put to death. But his charismatic presence returned to his disciples shortly after his crucifixion, and even after those vivid appearances ceased, it remained in a spiritual form that could be experienced by those who had never met him in the flesh.

Jesus' personal charisms were many. He spoke with a personal authority which commanded attention, and the things he said struck people as a revelation rather than as a repetition of what they already knew. He touched people both physically and spiritually, and through that touch their bodies were healed and their spirits were lifted. He acted sometimes decisively and sometimes enigmatically, seemingly sure of what he was doing but not always understood even by his disciples. His lifestyle testified to a transcendent richness which more than compensated for its worldly poverty. His behavior bore witness to a depth of reality which was not disturbed by the surface events of daily life. His prayer seemed to both grow out of and intensify his intimate relation with the God he addressed as *Abba*. Even his personality was charismatic, for to his followers it was obvious that the Spirit of God and the spirit of Jesus were one and the same.[14]

In this broad sense, then, Jesus was a sacramental person. His preaching announced that the reign of Satan was over and the reign of God had begun; and his life was a sign that this was true. What he said spoke God's word in the hearts

---

[14]See, for example, Donald Senior, C.P., *Jesus: A Gospel Portrait* Dayton, Ohio: Pflaum/Standard, 1975; Bruce Vawter, C.M., *This Man Jesus*, (New York: Doubleday, 1973).

of his hearers, and what he did revealed God's action in a world that often seemed anything but sacred. Jesus' concern for others was a sign of God's care for his people; his miracles were a sign of God's power and providence; his forgiveness of their sins was a sign of God's love, even — or rather especially — for sinners. Thus Jesus was a living symbol of salvation. To the poor he promised wealth; to the sorrowing he revealed reasons for joy ; to the blind he gave sight; to the discouraged he brought good news. The ultimate symbol of that salvation was Jesus' resurrection by the Father, for through his being raised he became a sign that those who lived in God had nothing to fear from death.[15]

We can say, therefore, that the first phase of Christian sacramentality was the *personal sacramentality* of Jesus himself: both the incarnate sacramentality of Jesus of Nazareth during his life time, and the transcendent sacramentality of Jesus the Christ after his resurrection. Moreover, Jesus' many charisms continued to be incarnated in the community of those who accepted his lordship over their lives. His disciples preached the good news of salvation from sin and death. Their fellowship was a living symbol of freedom from alienation and antagonism. Their ministering to each other's needs was a sign of how Christ wanted them to live, and their forgiveness of each other's faults was a sign of how he wanted them to love one another. This is not to say that the early Christian community was a perfect sacrament of Christ either for its own members or to the society in which it found itself. In both the Acts of the Apostles and the epistles of St. Paul, for example, we see not only the ideal sacramentality to which Christians were committed but also the failure of Christians to live up to that ideal.[16] But the ideal was none the less real in the minds and hearts

---

[15]See "Jesus as Figure and Person, Symbol and Sacrament" in Ann and Barry Ulanov, *Religion and the Unconscious* (Philadelphia: Westminster Press, 1975) pp. 97-117; Gerald O'Collins, S.J., *The Resurrection of Jesus Christ* (Valley Forge, Pennsylvania: Judson Press, 1973).

[16]See, for example, Acts 4:32-5:16; Rom. 6:1-4; 1 Cor. 11:17-34; Eph. 17:6-9.

and actions of those for whom Jesus was the way, the truth and the life.

This second phase of Christian sacramentality can be designated as a *charismatic sacramentality*, and this for a number of reasons. It was charismatic in Weber's sense that it was inspired by the charisma of Jesus, and that it began to routinize or repeat the types of charismatic behavior which characterized Jesus' life and made him a sacrament of God. It was also charismatic in the sense that the apostolic Church did many things which are typical of modern pentecostal churches and which are also found in the Catholic charismatic renewal: laying on of hands, speaking in tongues, prophesying in God's name, and so on.[17] But the sacramentality of the earliest Christian community was also charismatic in the sense that it tended to be spontaneous and "moved by the Spirit" rather than highly structured and organized. People were preached to wherever they were encountered; needs were met as they arose; ministers were sometimes chosen by lot, while at other times they were designated because they had the needed gifts (charisms) for the job. Jewish Christian communities tended to organize themselves in ways that Jews were used to; Hellenistic communities chose patterns that Greeks were more comfortable with. And through the course of the first century church structures and practices changed and evolved, not always in the same direction, and not always at the same pace.[18]

3. The Patristic Period

Even from the very beginning, however, there were a few ritual actions which seemed to be common to all Christian communities even though the apostolic Church was not

---

[17]See Acts 8:14-17; 10:44-48; 1 Cor. 12:8-11, 28-30; 14:1-40. John Koenig, *Charismata* (Philadelphia: Westminster Press, 1978) esp. ch. 2; Wade H. Horton, ed., *The Glossolalia Phenomenon* (Cleveland, Tennessee: Pathway Press, 1966) pp. 23-82.

[18]See Edward Schillebeeckx, O.P., *Ministry* (New York: Crossroad, 1981) ch. 1;

concerned with ritualism as such.[19] Those who became believers in Jesus were almost always initiated into their new life through a ritual immersion in water, or baptism. Christians often had hands laid on them while others prayed that they might receive the Holy Spirit, or that they might be spiritually strengthened or physically healed, or that they might worthily perform a ministry to which they were being called. And every community regularly shared the Lord's Supper, commemorating Jesus' last meal with his disciples, symbolizing the messianic banquet in the kingdom of God, and signifying the unity which they both desired and to some extent already experienced.

In these ritual routinizations of the charismatic spirit of Christ can be seen the emergence of a third type or phase of Christian sacramentality. It can be designated as a *communal sacramentality* because it was common to all the small and scattered Christian communities that were appearing around the Roman Empire, and because it began to form a focus for the communal life of those churches. Instead of baptisms being performed on the spot at the time of an individual's conversion, they came to be performed regularly at Easter or Pentecost, in the company of others who had accepted the Christian message, and in the presence of the head of the local congregation. Likewise the Lord's Supper by the third century was no longer a meal with other food besides bread and wine, but a more strictly symbolic meal that could be shared by the whole community even when the threat of persecution made meeting times short, and even when groups grew large enough that they could no longer fit around a common table for a full dinner. As these rituals took shape, therefore, both the yearly baptism and the weekly Eucharist became socially institutionalized forms of Christian sacramentality through which people

Eduard Schweizer, *Church Order in the New Testament* (London: SCM Press, 1961); James Mohler, *The Origin and Evolution of the Priesthood* (New York: Alba House, 1970).

[19]"Ritualism is taken to be a concern that efficacious symbols be correctly manipulated and that the right words be pronounced in the right order." Mary Douglas, *Natural Symbols* (New York: Vintage Books, 1973) p. 28.

were received into and celebrated their life within the Church.[20]

It was not until the fourth century that the next phase of Christian sacramentality began to appear as a distinct sacramental style. When Christianity was legalized and later made the official religion of the Roman Empire, it became necessary to move beyond the loosely structured rituals which had been characteristic of the earlier times. Besides having a more or less set pattern, Christian rituals began to be given definite contents in the form of words to be repeated and actions to be performed in one way and not another. Prayers began to get written down and reused, and rubrics began to be established as legal norms. When Sunday was declared an official day of rest (it had been just another weekday) the Eucharistic meal developed into an elaborate liturgy lasting up to three or four hours. Similarly, baptism moved from private homes and rain cisterns to basilicas and baptistries, and in doing so it became a more lengthy and formal process that began with prayers and exorcisms six weeks before Easter, continued with instructions and examinations during Holy Week, and culminated in the washing and anointing on the night of the Paschal Vigil.[21]

By the start of the patristic period, other charisms of Christ had already become routinized to some extent: healing, forgiveness, and service to others. Now, at the height of Mediterranean Christianity these too became connected with rituals of the institutional Church. Oil, water and other substances which were used for healing were sometimes blessed expressly for this purpose. The need to readmit repentant Christians who had renounced their faith during persecution led to the development of a "second baptism" or penitential discipline. When the persecutions were over, this

---

[20]See Arthur McCormack, *Christian Initiation* (New York: Hawthorn Books, 1969) ch. 3; Edward Kilmartin, S.J., *The Eucharist in the Primitive Church* (Englewood Cliffs, New Jersey: Prentice Hall, 1965).

[21]See O.C. Edwards, Jr., *How it All Began* (New York: Seabury Press, 1973); Martos, pp. 168-171; 247-53.

ecclesiastical ritual was also made available to notorious sinners who wanted to be reconciled with the community, and public penance became a process as lengthy as baptism but even more rigorous. Finally, certain forms of service became increasingly institutionalized as the Church grew in numbers and complexity. There developed specialized ministries of local church leadership (bishop), advising the bishop and later acting for him at Eucharist (presbyter), admistration of ecclesiastical and social services (deacon), secretarial duties (acolyte), caring for the needs of women (widows), instructing new converts during their preparation for baptism (teachers), and so on. And initiation into some of these services, especially the ministries of church leadership and liturgical worship, developed into institutional rituals which usually included a laying on of hands and a prayer over the candidates.[22]

During the period from the second through the sixth centuries, then, the Christian gifts of conversion and worship, forgiveness and service became not only routinized but also institutionalized in formal, set rituals. The patristic period may therefore be designated as the period of *institutional sacramentality*, for it was characterized by the establishment of repeated, authoritatively sanctioned actions which were instituted to continue certain charismatic activities of Christ within the world. This does not deny that there were also other non-ritualized ways of continuing the work of Christ (for example, teaching and preaching) and even non-institutionalized ways of doing this (for example, caring for the poor, or forgiving one another). Nor does it suggest that at this phase in the development of Christian sacramentality ritualism (in the technical sense of close attention to fixed rituals) was paramount. True, ritualism was growing, but through most of the patristic period there was still a great deal of regional diversity in ecclesiastical

---

[22]See Margaret Hebbelthwaite and Kevin Donovan, S.J., *The Theology of Penance* (Butler, Wisconsin: Clergy Book Service, 1979) ch. 2. Paul Edwards, S.J., *The Theology of the Priesthood* (Butler, Wisconsin: Clergy Book Service, 1974) chs. 3 and 4.

practices, and there was still much creative adaptation of church rituals to express the Christian mysteries and to meet the people's spiritual needs.

4. The Medieval Period

The time between the fall of Rome (around 500) and the end of the Viking raids on southern Europe (around 1000) is sometimes called the Dark Ages because it was not a time of great intellectual enlightenment. It was nevertheless a time of cultural transition and many practical changes in the Church. With the loss of North Africa and the Middle East to the Moslem Empire, and with its growing isolation from the Greek churches, European Christianity became Germanic rather than Mediterranean in culture. Moreover, the Germanic tribes which overran and pillaged Europe were pre-agricultural peoples whose religion was of the primitive rather than the classical type. And so even when they settled down and accepted Christianity as their religion, they brought into it many of their own cultural attitudes and practices. Principal among these, from the viewpoint of a history of sacramentality, was a belief in the automatic effectiveness of ritual.

To some extent all rituals are automatically effective. Like signs or symbols of any sort, rituals seem to signify things and bring about changes without any deliberate effort on the part of the participants. Moreover, people are not ordinarily aware of how their personal commitments and social presuppositions contribute to the effectiveness of their rituals. Thus even in the institutional sacramentality of the patristic world there was a tendency to speak about rituals having certain effects quite independently of the ministers and the recipients. Theologically it was understood that God caused the effects and that the rituals were just the means through which he acted in a hidden yet real way on the soul.

The prime example of this was baptism. Initially it had

been a process of personal conversion and commitment, symbolized and finally effected by a ritual of bathing, anointing, dressing in new clothing, and sharing food wtih one's new community. By late patristic times it had become a brief ritual for infants symbolizing the washing away of original sin and effecting one's entrance into the Church. Then, when this abbreviated ritual was used to symbolize a tribe's acceptance of Christianity, sometimes hundreds of adults were baptized with little or no preparation, and they were told that as a result of this ritual their past sins were all forgiven. Likewise they were told that their children, in order to join the Church and be saved, had to be dipped in or sprinkled with water while certain words in a strange language (Latin) were recited.[23]

Also illustrative of this attitude toward sacraments was what happened when confirmation became a separate sacrament. Following the practice of Rome, Germanic bishops commonly reserved the anointing after baptism to themselves; but this meant that children were regularly baptized by local priests and not anointed until some time later when the bishop could visit their locality. The existence of this separate ritual naturally led some to wonder about its effects. Since this anointing had no obvious experiential or social effects, theologians looked to the scriptures for clues about possible hidden, spiritual effects. Eventually it was agreed that the Holy Spirit was received more fully than in baptism, and that through the ritual Christians were strengthened to overcome the trials of adult life.[24]

Much the same can be seen in the evolution of extreme unction. Even before the Middle Ages both priests and lay people had anointed the sick in the hope that God's healing power might be communicated through the oil and bring about recovery. Around the ninth century, however, this

---

[23]On this period and on baptism in particular, see Martos, pp. 167-183; also Alexander Ganoczy, *Becoming Christian* (New York: Paulist Press, 1976).

[24]See Austin Milner, O.P., *The Theology of Confirmation* (Butler, Wisconsin: Clergy Book Service, 1972) ch. 2; Jean-Paul Bouhot, *La Confirmation* (Paris: Éditions du Chalet, 1968) pp. 66-90.

anointing came to be administered only in cases of very severe illness. But if this anointing no longer effected physical recovery, it seemed that its effects must be purely spiritual. Gradually both the prayers that accompanied the ritual and the theology that explained it reflected the growing belief that its hidden effect was to prepare the soul of the recipient for heaven. And since those who received the sacrament were sometimes at the point of death and even unconscious, it seemed natural to believe that the ritual had to be automatically effective.[25]

For a long time those who oversaw the Church's penitential practices resisted this tendency towards automatic effectiveness. Until the ninth century harsh penances had to be performed *before* a sinner would be readmitted to communion, and after the penance was done the priest prayed *asking* that God would forgive his sins. By the eleventh century, however, it was becoming common for people to perform less severe penances *after* being readmitted to the altar, and it was becoming customary for priests to *declare* that the sins had been absolved. Thus from the twelfth century onward penance was considered to be automatically effective, with God's grace coming through the priestly ritual —even though in this case (as also with the other sacraments) people had to be predisposed to accepting that grace and cooperating with it.[26]

During the medieval period, therefore, *ritual sacramentality* became the dominant mode or style of Christian religious practice. Ordination quite easily lent itself to this interpretation since it had always been true that the ceremony marked the beginning of a man's priestly ministry.[27]

---

[25] See in this series, James L. Empereur, S.J., *Prophetic Anointing* (Wilmington, Delaware: Michael Glazier, 1982) ch. 1; Claude Ortemann, *Le Sacrement des Malades* (Paris: Éditions du Chalet, 1971) pp. 27-57.

[26] See in this series, Monika Hellwig, *Sign of Reconciliation and Conversion* (Wilmington, Delaware: Michael Glazier, 1982) chs. 4-5.

[27] On the shift from institutional to ritual sacramentality regarding ordination, see in this series, Nathan Mitchell, O.S.B., *Mission and Ministry* (Wilmington, Delaware: Michael Glazier, 1982) ch. 4.

Quite literally, the ordination ritual made a man a priest. And when matrimony became an ecclesiastical ritual around the twelfth century (before this it had been either a private agreement between the man and woman, or a family ceremony usually presided over by the father of the bride) it was easy to perceive the bond of mariage as a hidden effect resulting from the performance of the wedding ceremony.[28]

By the later Middle Ages this attitude so pervaded the Catholic sacraments that even the Mass was commonly regarded as having a number of automatic effects. Chief among these, of course, was the "confecting" (as it was sometimes called) of Christ's body and blood out of bread and wine. But the Mass was also regarded as a sacrifice which took place every time the Eucharist was offered to God, and the spiritual merits of this sacrifice were believed to be applicable to whomever the priest intended. In addition, popular superstition attributed magical powers to the consecrated host and magical effects to its worship.

What was happening was that ritual sacramentality was becoming divorced from institutional sacramentality and connected to individual initiative on the part of both the ministers and the recipients. Similarly the sacraments became only tenuously attached to any aspect of communal sacramentality while becoming more and more associated with personal piety. Finally, insistence on the notion that God guaranteed the effectiveness of the rituals regardless of whether or not any effects were felt led to an almost total loss of the charismatic dimensions of the sacraments. Nevertheless, the sacraments were still theologically related to the sacramentality of Jesus through the understanding that Christ acted in the sacraments and had personally instituted all seven of them.

---

[28]On the development of the medieval wedding ritual and scholastic theology, see Edward Schillebeeckx, O.P., *Marriage* (New York: Sheed and Ward, 1965) pp. 272-332.

5. The Tridentine Period[29]

Although there were in fact many reasons why Martin Luther and the other reformers rejected the ritual sacramentality of medieval Catholicism, theologically it can be said that they found unintelligible and intolerable a style of saramentality which had little or no inner effect on people, which was separated from the communal life of the Church, and which was even lacking proper institutional regulation. They accepted, however, the Catholic belief in the sacraments' institution by Christ, and using the Bible rather than custom as a guide for determining which of the sacraments actually came from Jesus, they acknowledged baptism and Eucharist (which are both explicitly mentioned in the scriptures) as genuine sacraments and regarded the other five as ecclesiastical inventions. They also accepted the traditional belief that Christ acted through these sacraments, even though they came to disagree among themselves as to how the divine activity was accomplished in these two cases.[30]

Within the Protestant vision of Christian sacramentality can be seen the beginning of a shift toward a more modern mentality. By and large it grew out of a dissatisfaction with the ritualism of the Middle ages and expressed a desire for a more integrated personal involvement in sacramental actions. On the one hand Protestantism insisted that God's action in the world could not be confined to ecclesiastical rituals; but on the other hand it equally insisted on the importance of an active faith and a personal response to God when he did act through the sacraments. To some extent the pluralism of Protestant practices and interpretations of the sacraments came out of a constant search by various denominations to find new sacramental forms

---

[29]In *Doors to the Sacred* I refer to this as the *modern* period, following the usage of literature and the arts. Following Bellah's usage of the term, however, Christianity began to develop a modern cultural style with early Protestantism, but Catholicism has begun to enter the modern phase of religion only in the second half of the twentieth century.

[30]See G.W. Bromiley, *Sacramental Teaching and Practice in the Reformation Churches* (Grand Rapids, Michigan: William B. Eerdmans, 1957).

which would allow God's presence and power to be experienced, acknowledge and lived.

In response to the Protestant Reformation, the Council of Trent (1545-63) initiated a Catholic counter-reformation which first of all insisted on the traditional numbering of the sacraments as seven. It found references in the New Testament to all of them, and even though it could not find an explicit record of Christ having instituted each of them, it reasoned that God need not have given the Church a written record if he made them a part of the Church's institutional practice. Secondly, the council reaffirmed the medieval theology of the sacraments as an intellectually valid way of explaining what they were and how God acted through them. Even though this scholastic theology was sometimes misunderstood, the council reasoned, it provided a sound philosophical framework for understanding their place in the life of the Church and their role in effecting the salvation of individuals. Thirdly, it acknowledged the truth of the reformers' charges that the Church's sacramental system was open to many practical abuses, and it initiated a series of reforms designed to eliminate most of them. By insisting on better theological training for priests, by eliminating much of the laxity in church government, and by tightening the regulations for the proper performance of the sacramental rituals, the Council of Trent and the popes who came after it were able to ensure that there was a closer correspondence between sacramental theology and sacramental practice.[31]

During the Tridentine period, therefore, the Catholic Church developed what might be called a *purified* or *stabilized ritual sacramentality*. It was a purified sacramentality because it was purged of many practices which had obscured the theological meaning of the sacraments and which had often vitiated their spiritual value. But it was also a stabilized sacramentality because for the first time in Chris-

---

[31] See Philip Hughes, *The Church in Crisis* (New York: Doubleday, 1961) ch. 19; Henri Daniel-Rops, *The Catholic Reformation* (London: J.M. Dent, 1962) pp. 79-104.

tian history the sacraments were given a uniform set of rites which were to be used in the entire Church and which were not to be altered without explicit permission from Rome. In this way Catholicism reintroduced and reinforced the institutional dimension of sacramentality in its liturgical worship, and in authoritatively sanctioning the specific rituals the magisterium guaranteed that these were indeed instruments of salvation and channels of grace. But as a church Catholicism did not retrieve the communal or charismatic aspects of the sacraments, for there is not much evidence of these in either the theology or the canon law of this period. This is not to deny, however, that there were communal dimensions to local celebrations of the sacraments,[32] or that there were charismatic ministers of the sacraments.[33] But it does affirm that the main emphasis in both theology and practice was on the institutional and ritual aspects of the sacraments.

6. The Contemporary Period

Since the Second Vatican Council in the 1960s, the Church has entered a new phase in its sacramental life. Most Catholics associate this new phase with the liturgical reforms of the 1970s (liturgy in vernacular languages, a variety of rites for a number of sacraments, and so forth). Some also associate it with the new theological outlook (based on personalism, existentialism and phenomenology) that replaced scholasticism (based on ancient Greek philosophy and medieval metaphysics) during the same period, Both the liturgical reforms and the theological shift, however, are merely part of a vast transformation of Catholicism which has, in fact, just begun. The present cultural

---

[32] I am thinking of the role that daily Mass would play in the community life of a convent, for example, and of parish celebrations such as baptisms, first communion, and weddings.

[33] For example, the Curé of Ars was renowned as a holy and insightful confessor; others could also be mentioned.

transformation of the Catholic religion is more sweeping than changes in sacramental rituals and it runs deeper than changes in sacramental theology.[34]

In regard to the sacraments, however, it encompasses a retrieval of all the previous phases of Christian sacramentality, a recognition that they are all important for worship, and a projection of all of them simultaneously into the future. Just as developmental psychology recognized that each succeeding stage in personal development incorporates, modifies and builds upon the preceding stages of individual growth, so also sociology and history recognize that each succeeding stage in cultural evolution builds upon the preceding stages of social development. Normally, as we look back at our past life or our collective history we notice only the new things that emerged at each step along the way, but modern psychology, sociology and history make us aware that the past is still with us. And insofar as we can rediscover the past and affirm that it is truly part of us (instead of denying it the way an adolescent denies his childhood, or the way "modern" Catholics reject the "old" Church), we can be more fully aware of what we have become and allow ourselves to be any or all of them in the future.

This kind of self awareness and self consciousness involves both differentiation and integration. The differentiation is a matter of discovering and distinguishing the various components which make up the present reality (whether that reality is our individual personality, or secular society, or the Church). The integration is a matter of acknowledging the contribution and worth of the various components, and then approving their successive or simultaneous interaction (as individuals we alternate between different emotional states, realms of meaning, and so forth, for example; as a society we tolerate ethnic diversity, encourage occupational diversification, allow for political differences, and so forth). This same sort of differentiation

---

[34]On this point, see Martos, ch. 5, and sec. 5 of chs. 6-12.

has already occurred in the area of the sacraments; and this same sort of integration is already beginning.

The differentiation can be discerned in the various intellectual and practical movements that have had an impact on the sacraments during the past half century or so. The Catholic biblical revival which began in the forties and fifties with scholarly research and scientific methods of interpretation eventually led to a reawakened appreciation of the sacramentality of Christ. Patristic studies which had begun even earlier quickly went beyond initial attempts to verify the existence of the sacraments in ancient Christianity and discovered the regional diversity of sacramental forms which flourished in that period of institutional sacramentality. For if the Church itself is a sacrament, then it can actualize that sacramentality in a variety of institutional practices suited to diverse social needs and cultural styles. The liturgical renewal (which actually began, as has been noted, in the last century) revivified the Catholic appreciation of ritual sacramentality by emphasizing the significance of symbolism in the words and gestures of the sacraments, and by insisting on the importance of liturgical vestments and church architecture. The ecumenical movement that followed Vatican II led Catholics to acknowledge the soundness of Protestant insights into the simultaneous immanence and transcendence of God's action in sacraments, and into the need for a personal response in faith on the part of those who participate in them. The charismatic renewal in the Church has allowed many to rediscover the charismatic dimension of sacramental spirituality. Philosophical developments such as existentialism which emphasizes personal responsibility and decisive action, and such as Marxism which insists on an integration of social ideology and social praxis, have led to a greater appreciation of the personal sacramentality of each Christian as a witness to others, and to a greater awareness of the communal sacramentality of the local church as a testimony to Christ in the midst of secular society. The contemporary Catholic understanding of sacramentality has therefore been both broadened and deepened through the research and reflection of many scholars and specialists who have retrieved the many dimensions of sacramentality in the past, and who have at the same time made each of those dimensions explicit and available in the present.

It can be anticipated, then, that the modern phase of Catholic sacramentality, as it unfolds in the future, will not be a new culturally uniform type of spirituality, for the Church is moving out of a period of cultural uniformity (that is, identification with European culture) and into a period of cultural diversity (that is, identification with many regional cultures around the globe). Even less will it be a reversion to one of the previous phases of Christian sacramentality (despite the sometimes narrow enthusiasm of liturgical purists, charismatic communities, traditionalist movements, and so on). Rather, modern Catholicism will embrace all of the previous phases as dimensions of its own catholic sacramentality: a sacramentality which in the past spanned centuries of change and development, but which in the future will encompass continents of cultural diversity.

Modern Catholic sacramentality can therefore be designated as *pluralistic sacramentality*, for it both acknowledges the sequential pluralism of the past and looks forward to the simultaneous pluralism of the future. The period in which we find ourselves is therefore still a transitional stage, for although the differentiation of the various aspects of sacramentality is well under way, its integration has only just begun.

Individually that integration will ultimately mean less dissociation between religious beliefs and our everyday lives, and more connectedness between what we live from day to day and what we celebrate in the sacraments. Communally that integration will mean less alienation between individuals and more cooperation in a unity which is both expressed and fostered in group worship. Ecclesiologically that integration will mean less cultural hegemony and ritual uniformity at the expense of other cultures and other possible ritual forms, and more tolerance, appreciation and encouragement for a sacramental pluriformity fitted to the needs of diverse cultures and specialized groups. Theologically that integration will mean less of an attempt to develop a single over-arching sacramental theology and more attempts by individuals and groups to develop sacramental theologies which are integral with their own experience of themselves, God and the Church, and with their own understanding of the scriptures, the world and history.

Recommended Reading

In addition to the other volumes in this series, all of which treat the historical aspects of their respective sacraments, very readable accounts of sacramental development may be found in the following works:

Lorna Brockett, R.S.C.J., *The Theology of Baptism* (Butler, Wisconsin: Clergy Book Service, 1971).

Austin Milner, O.P., *The Theology of Confirmation* (Butler, Wisconsin: Clergy Book Service, 1972).

Josef A. Jungmann, S.J., *The Mass* (Collegeville, Minnesota: Liturgical Press, 1976).

Theorore Klauser, *A Short History of the Western Liturgy* (London: Oxford University Press, 1969).

Margaret Hebbelthwaite and Kevin Donovan, S.J., *The Theology of Penance* (Butler, Wisconsin: Clergy Book Service, 1979).

Rosemary Haughton, *The Theology of Marriage* (Butler, Wisconsin: Clergy Book Service, 1971).

Paul Edwards, S.J., *The Theology of the Priesthood* (Butler, Wisconsin: Clergy Book Service, 1974).

Joseph Martos, *Doors to the Sacred: A Historical Introduction to Sacraments in the Catholic Church* (New York: Doubleday, 1981).

To situate the changes in the sacraments within the larger picture of theological development, the following are helpful:

Yves Congar, O.P., *A History of Theology* (New York: Doubleday, 1968).

Jaroslav Pelikan, *The Christian Tradition: A History of the Development of Doctrine* (Chicago: University of Chicago Press, 3 vols. 1971-78).

Justo L. Gonzalez, *A History of Christian Thought* (Nashville: Abingdon Press, 3 vols. 1970-75).

CHAPTER IV: THEOLOGY AND THE SACRAMENTS

The sacraments did not always have a theology. If sacramental theology is a sustained reflection on sacramental practice and experience in the light of scripture and tradition, then we must admit that that sort of product did not exist in the early Church. This is not to say that the early Christians did not understand what they were doing when they shared the Lord's Supper, when they baptized, or when they laid hands on people. But it was not until later in the patristic period that some of the Church fathers began to offer somewhat theoretical explanations of what the sacraments were and how they worked.

Moreover, it was not until the Middle Ages that Catholic theologians developed a single, systematic way of understanding what today we call the seven ecclesial sacraments. The sacramental theology of the scholastics, based on the philosophical system of Aristotle, gave Christianity a more or less unified sacramental theory which, despite differences among the doctrines of Thomas Aquinas, Hugh of St. Victor, John Duns Scotus and others, provided a common framework for understanding the nature and function of the sacraments.[1]

---

[1] For a handy sketch of the history of sacramental theology, see J.R. Quinn, "Sacramental Theology," *New Catholic Encyclopedia* (New York: McGraw Hill,

Scholastic concepts provided the only acceptable Catholic explanation for the sacraments until the twentieth century. Today, however, scholasticism is regarded as but one possible philosophical system among many, and so instead of there being a single Catholic sacramental theology there is a growing variety of sacramental theologies.

1. Theological Developments Affecting the Sacraments

The idea that there can be different ways of understanding the sacraments seems strange to Catholics who grew up with a Tridentine mentality. The Council of Trent in the sixteenth century and the Church's magisterium since then repeatedly warned Catholics against entertaining other than the scholastic explanations of the sacraments.[2]

It is important to remember, however, that even within our own tradition (that is, not including the Eastern Orthodox and Protestant traditions) there is indeed a pluralism in Catholic theology. It may be called a *sequential pluralism* since there has been a succession of theologies and theological styles through the course of the centuries. The ways that the apostolic community understood its sacramental actions was somewhat different from the ways that the fathers of the Church understood them. The earliest Christians had an implicit understanding of what they were doing and what God was doing in their sacramental practices, and this implicit understanding got expressed both in the prayers and other words which accompanied the physical gestures, and — to some extent, at least — in the gospels

---

1966) Vol. XII, p. 789f. Scholastic presentations of sacramental theology can be found in Clarence McAuliffe, S.J., *Sacramental Theology* (St. Louis: B. Herder Book Company, 1958); Ludwig Ott, *Fundamentals of Catholic Dogma* (Cork, Ireland: Mercer Press, 1955).

[2]For excerpts from conciliar and papal documents on the sacraments, see *The Church Teaches: Documents of the Church in English Translation* (St. Louis: B. Herder Book Company, 1955) pp. 257-344; also Ott, Part IV,2.

and epistles of the New Testament. This implicit understanding also got expressed in sermons and essays which bishops wrote to explain the sacramental rituals for converts, for their congregations, and for the sake of refuting heresies. At the start, these explanations were very scriptural in tone and language, but eventually they became more metaphysical, adopting the language of the Greek philosophers Plato and Plotinus. Still, the fathers' explicitation of their implicit understanding of the sacraments was often more practical than theoretical in intent, and it was often more pastoral than systematic in approach.[3]

Even in scholasticism there is sometimes a noticeable difference between the interpretations of sacraments given by the early schoolmen and those given by the later schoolmen and the neo-scholastics. In discussing penance, for example, Peter Abelard in the twelfth century gave much more importance to psychological factors such as shame and remorse than did John Duns Scotus in the thirteenth century in his more legalistic approach to the sacraments. Early scholasticism still mentioned physical healing as a possible effect of extreme unction, but late scholasticism regarded the sacrament almost exclusively as a preparation for death. Some of the earliest schoolmen even doubted whether marriage should be classified as a sacrament.[4]

In addition, the more we learned about earlier periods of Catholic history, the more we realized that prior to the period of Tridentine uniformity, there was a greater variety in the sacramental theories of patristic and medieval writers than had been previously recognized. The relative isolation of cultural centers and the slowness of copying and transporting theological works resulted in a high degree of intel-

---

[3] A standard reference work for patristic sources is Johannes Quasten, *Patrology* (Westminster, Maryland: Newman Press, 3 vols. 1963). On the sacraments specifically, see J. N. D. Kelly, *Early Christian Doctrines* (London: Adam and Charles Black, 1958) ch. 16.

[4] For these and other examples, see Joseph Martos, *Doors to the Sacred* (New York: Doubleday, 1981), as well as the historical treatments of the sacraments in the other volumes in this series.

lectual individualism even when the basic style of theologizing was fairly uniform.[5]

The essential difference, then, between the present period of Catholic theology and the previous period is not that in the past there was agreement and today there is disagreement. Rather, it is first of all that in the past there was a sequential pluralism of approaches whereas today we are entering a period of *simultaneous pluralism*. And secondly it is that in the past the slowness of communication and the relative isolation of regions insured that theological differences often went unrecognized,[6] whereas today differences are not only recognized but even to some extent encouraged.

To be sure, it has taken a while for modern Catholicism to adopt this culturally modern attitude toward sacramental theology. One of the first persons to offer an alternative to the standard scholastic approach to the sacraments was Dom Odo Casel, a Benedictine monk in the monastery of Maria Laach. Casel was a leading figure in the liturgical movement in Germany who tried to develop a sacramental theology which deliberately took active participation in the liturgy and the experience of mystery in Christian worship as its foundation. His ideas, though never condemned by the magisterium, were long regarded with official suspicion and unofficial scepticism, and it was not until the late 1950s that his originality began to be fully appreciated.[7]

As was noted in the first section of the previous chapter, it

---

[5]For a glimpse of this variety, see Paul F. Palmer, S.J., ed., *Sources of Christian Theology* (Westminster, Maryland: Newman Press), Vol. I, *Sacraments and Worship* (1955), Vol. II, *Sacraments and Forgiveness* (1959).

[6]Heretical differences were of course recognized, but these were not included *within* orthodox theology. The general tendency was either to ignore the divergent views of other theologians or to harmonize what they wrote with one's own position. A good example of this latter practice is the way St. Thomas Acquinas used quotations from patristic writers in his own *Summa Theologica*.

[7]For summaries of Casel's contribution, read the articles by Burkhard Neunheuser and Charles Davis in *Worship* 34(1960) pp. 120-127 and 428-438; see also Odo Casel, *The Mystery of Christ, and Other Writings* (Westminster, Maryland: Newman Press, 1962).

was also during this period following the Second World War that the liturgical movement began to gain momentum, partly as a result of the research that had been going on into the history of Catholic worship. That research made it clear that Christian sacramental life had been understood in other ways before the advent of medieval scholasticism, and so it opened Catholic thinkers to the possibility of explaining the sacraments in non-scholastic terms. And the desire to do this was heightened still further by the rapid expansion of Catholic biblical studies during the 1950s. Scripture scholars were discovering that scholastic philosophical categories were often ill suited for interpreting what the Bible was saying, and so systematic theologians began to search for other philosophical systems which might provide a better intellectual framework for their discussion of revelation.[8]

They found what they were looking for, at least initially, in contemporary existentialism and phenomenology, two sometimes overlapping philosophical methods which emphasized the examining of concrete human realities and which focused on the experience of being a person. Although neither philosophy was explicitly religious (some of their leading proponents were avowedly agnostic or atheistic), Catholic theologians discovered that they could use existential thinking and phenomenological analysis to examine concrete religious realities such as faith, and to explore the experience of being a Christian.

Foremost among the Catholic scholars who began to use these philosophical methods as an intellectual foundation for their own theologizing about the sacraments were Edward Schillebeeckx in Holland and Karl Rahner in Germany. In 1952 Schillebeeckx published *De sacramentele Heilseconomie (The Sacramental Economy of Salvation)*, in which he examined the traditional scholastic theology of the sacraments from a historical, doctrinal and theological

---

[8]See Elmer O'Brien, S.J., *Theology in Transition* (New York: Herder and Herder, 1965) esp. pp. 174-211. Also, T.M. Schoof, *A Survey of Catholic Theology, 1800-1970* (New York: Paulist Press, 1970) presents the broader context for these developments on pp. 121-224.

perspective. He was careful, moreover, not to deny the validity of the traditional explanation of salvation and the sacraments, and in 1957 he showed the compatibility of existentialist and scholastic categories in *Christ, the Sacrament of the Encounter with God*. Rahner's broad philosophical framework may be termed neoscholasticism or transcendental Thomism, but it grew partly out of a thoroughgoing attempt to integrate the valid insights of scholasticism with the philosophical analyses of Martin Heidegger. In his short work, *The Church and the Sacraments*, Rahner showed that he too, like Schillebeeckx, was concerned with providing a more contemporary philosophical foundation for traditional sacramental theology.

As the work of scripture scholars, church historians, liturgical experts and philosophical theologians found its way into Catholic thinking about the sacraments, there occurred what can only be called a massive shift in sacramental theology. Scriptural studies forced a reexamination of the belief that Christ had personally instituted each of the sacraments, but more importantly they suggested that the sacraments should be studied not within abstract treatments of supernatural grace but within the concrete context of salvation history and the redemption wrought by Christ's death and resurrection.[9] Patristic and other historical studies suggested that sacraments had to be understood not as isolated acts of individuals but as communal events in the life of the church and as ecclesial participations in the priesthood of Christ.[10] Liturgical studies indicated that a more adequate appreciation of the sacraments necessitated a whole series of shifts from attendance to participation in the liturgy, from administration and reception of sacraments to celebrations of the Christian mysteries, and from a focus on

---

[9]See Francois-Xavier Durrwell, C.SS.R., *The Resurrection* (New York: Sheed and Ward, 1960) esp. ch. 8, and *In the Redeeming Christ* (New York: Sheed and Ward, 1963) esp. Part II.

[10]See Aimé Georges Martimort, *The Signs of the New Covenant* (Collegeville, Minnesota: Liturgical Press, 1963); Colman E. O'Neill, O.P., *Meeting Christ in the Sacraments* (New York: Alba House, 1964).

rubrics and validity to an awareness of dynamics and appropriateness.[11] Finally, both neoscholasticism and modern philosophies insisted that it was better to speak of sacraments as signs rather than causes of grace, in personalistic rather than mechanistic fashion, using experiential rather than metaphysical categories.[12]

Many of these themes were summed up in an influential little book by the then Catholic theologian, Charles Davis:

> Jesus is the centre of redemptive history; he has brought the decisive intervention of God; in him has been fulfilled the expectation of the Old Testament; his death and resurrection are the great central events of all time; salvation has been accomplished; all that went before led up to him, all that comes after depends on him.
>
> The liturgy is the mystery of Christ made present to us. It is a symbolic representation of the saving work of Christ in which the reality of that work becomes present ... insofar as it is reproduced in us by the present action of the risen Christ.
>
> The Church owes its existence to the mystery of Christ. It is founded on his death and resurrection. And its enduring existence is secured by the sacramental renewal of that mystery.[13]

For a while in the 1960s it seemed as though Catholic theologians had succeeded in combining the old and the new into a stable and satisfactory synthesis. In 1963 the Vatican

---

[11] See Massey H. Shepherd, ed., *The Liturgical Renewal of the Church* (New York: Oxford University Press, 1960) chs. 1 and 2; Lancelot Sheppard, trans., *The Liturgical Movement* (New York: Hawthorn Books, 1964).

[12] See John H. Miller, C.S.C., *Signs of Transformation in Christ* (Englewood Cliffs, New Jersey: Prentice Hall, 1963); C. Stephen Sullivan, F.S.C., ed., *Readings in Sacramental Theology* (Englewood Cliffs, New Jersey: Prentice Hall, 1964).

[13] Charles Davis, *Liturgy and Doctrine* (London: Sheed and Ward, 1964) p. 42, p. 73, p. 56.

Council's *Constitution on the Sacred Liturgy* called for an updating of the Church's sacramental life based in large measure on this broadened understanding of sacramental theology. For the remainder of the decade and well into the 1970s great efforts were put into the practical work of liturgical reform and the educational task of informing both clergy and laity about the nature and purpose of the revised rites.[14] And while these practical tasks were absorbing most of Catholicism's liturgical energies there seemed to be little forward movement in sacramental theory.

Unfortunately, however, neither the liturgical renewal nor the educational efforts of theologians and catechists had uniformly happy results. In many ways the liturgy became more meaningful, but Mass attendance dropped. The sometimes legalistic practice of penance became a more interpersonal process of reconciliation, but confession lines dwindled. Seminary and clerical life became less monastic, but vocations to the priesthood fell off. Marriage became viewed less as a contract and more as a covenant, but the divorce rate among Catholics increased.[15] So it was not long after the reforms had been put into effect that liturgists and theologians themselves began to wonder about the theology on which the reforms were based, and to look more deeply into the nature and purpose of sacraments.

The result is that "alternative" sacramental theologies, some of which attracted little attention when they were first published, are beginning to be examined more seriously. It is not that any one of them is becoming regarded as the "new" sacramental theology which will eventually replace

[14]For the complete texts and official introductions, see *The Rites of the Catholic Church* (New York: Pueblo Publishing Company, 2 vols., 1976, 1980) For commentaries on the new rites, see James D. Crichton, *Christian Celebrations: The Sacraments* (London: Geoffrey Chapman, 1973).

[15]Of course the changes in sacramental theology and practice did not in themselves cause these things to happen, but they did in some ways enable them to happen by suggesting that if official change is possible then unofficial change is also possible, and they certainly did not prevent these things from happening. For a good sampling of what theologians were thinking about the changes, one can read many of the articles in the liturgical journal, *Worship*, written during the 1960s and 70s.

the synthesis of the 1960s; rather, in a culturally more modern fashion, they are looked upon as diverse ways of interpreting the sacraments within a variety of theological contexts.

From the present variety of sacramental theologies we can of necessity take only a sampling. We shall begin with the scholastic approach since it has held such a central place in Catholic thought since the Middle Ages, even though it is no longer used as a philosophical base by contemporary sacramental theologians. After that, we shall take a brief look at the beginning of the shift away from this scholastic perspective towards a more pastoral approach taken by the bishops at the Second Vatican Council. Finally, we shall examine four contemporary approaches which illustrate the diversity of Catholic sacramental theology in the second half of the twentieth century. Other approaches to the sacraments are possible, and these four do not in themselves represent the attitudes of the authors of the other volumes in this series. On the contrary, they represent relatively "pure" cases of current perspectives on the sacraments, which therefore lend themselves to being summarized without becoming too distorted by simplifications which must necessarily sacrifice detail for conciseness and nuance for clarity.

2. The Scholastic Approach

The traditional theological context for understanding the sacraments in the Roman Catholic Church has been that of scholasticism, a system of ideas developed by men who taught in medieval universities and schools of theology. These schoolmen or scholastics, as they came to be known, used the writings of the Greek philosopher Aristotle as a basis for their systematic approach to understanding all of reality.[16] In areas such as physics and astronomy, biology

---

[16] As an introduction to this period, one may read Frederick Copleston, S.J., *A History of Medieval Philosophy* (London: Methuen, 1972); Philip Delhaye,

and anatomy, logic and psychology, ethics and politics, and so on, they often borrowed from Aristotle's ideas in a fairly straightforward manner, developing as they did so their own scholastic philosophy. But in discussing the Christian mysteries of the Trinity, grace, redemption, the Church, and the sacraments, they had to rethink much of what they found in Aristotle's metaphysics and integrate it with what they derived from the Christian tradition, to develop what became known as scholastic theology.[17]

Traditional scholasticism, however, was not a homogeneous synthesis of conclusions that all Catholic thinkers agreed to, for there were many details over which theologians disagreed. Rather, it embraced a unified set of assumptions about the way to approach theological questions, about the way to use the scriptures, the writings of the fathers, established doctrines, canon law and church practice, in order to arrive at a theoretical understanding of the Christian mysteries. The basic soundness of this theological method is attested to by the way it provided a foundation for Catholic theology for over seven centuries. Medieval thinkers such as Thomas Aquinas and John Duns Scotus, and later ones such as Francis Suarez and Cardinal Cajetan, all worked within the scholastic framework, as did most lesser known Catholic theologians. This framework was also adopted by the Council of Trent in the sixteenth century, which was convened to counteract the Protestant revolt, and which ushered in a long period of relative stability in all of Catholic theology, including sacramental theology.[18]

Despite differences in detail, then, the scholastic approach to the sacraments sanctioned by the Council of Trent worked with a fundamental set of key concepts which

---

Medieval Christian Philosophy (New York: Hawthorn, 1960); Josef Pieper, *Scholasticism* (London: Faber and Faber, 1960).

[17]See Yves Congar, O.P., *A History of Theology* (New York: Doubleday, 1968) chs. 3 and 4; also Martos, ch. 3, and sec. 3 of chs. 8 through 12.

[18]Because of the implicit approval that the council gave to this approach, scholastic theology is sometimes referred to as Tridentine theology.

were developed during the Middle Ages, and which provided an intellectual framework for explaining the meaning and purpose of the Church's sacramental worship. From an Aristotelian point of view, the Church is a "perfect society," which is to say that it has within it everything that is needed for its existence and for the fulfillment of its ends.[19] As a human society, the Church needs members and it needs order; but as a society whose ends are supernatural, the Church needs the means to bring its members, and indeed the whole world, to salvation. Thus Christ in founding the Church also instituted the sacraments as the means by which individuals become members of the Church (baptism), are strengthened by the Holy Spirit (confirmation), enter into communion with Christ (Eucharist), are forgiven for their sins (penance), and prepare for life hereafter (extreme unction). In addition, he provided two sacraments whose purpose is social rather than individual, one for the preservation of the family and the propagation of offspring (matrimony), and one for the governance of the Church and the continuation of the sacramental economy of salvation (holy orders). As can be easily imagined, this is a view of the sacramental system which made great sense in the relatively stable and simple life of the Middle Ages.

Moreover, if one uses Aristotelian categories to understand the essential nature of sacraments, they quite obviously fall under two categories, signs and causes. That they are signs is clear from the fact that they are not realities in themselves but indicators of unseen supernatural realities such as divine grace and forgiveness. That they are causes is equally clear from the fact, attested to by official doctrine and by the rites themselves, that they effect certain changes in the souls of individuals and have definite consequences for the life of the Church.[20] The sacraments are thus signs

---

[19]See Ott, p. 275f.

[20]I have tried to give a more complete account of why the sacraments were regarded as causes in the Aristotelian sense of that term in *Doors to the Sacred*, pp. 81-84.

which have supernatural effects: they are effective or efficacious signs.

But what is it that the sacraments cause? It is at this point that we reach the limits of Aristotelian metaphysics and must introduce a distinctly Christian category, namely grace.[21] In one sense, all good things are gifts from God, or graces, but more specifically Christian theology uses the term, grace, to refer to the gift of divine life which makes people morally good and able to lead holy lives. For this reason it is called sanctifying grace. It comes from God himself, either directly or through certain channels such as the sacraments. Sacraments are thus instrumental causes of grace, and evidence of this can be seen in the fact that the basic way that Christians achieve holiness is by being baptized and confirmed in the Church, by going to confession and the Mass regularly, and by entering into a particular state of life through matrimony or holy orders. All sacraments therefore confer sanctifying grace, but in addition each sacrament confers a supernatural strengthening which enables the recipient to be holy in a specific way, such as avoiding a confessed sin (penance), or such as being a devoted spouse (matrimony).

Now if sacraments are instrumental causes of grace (God being the primary cause), it follows that the sacramental rituals themselves, not the ministers who perform them, are the channels through which the effects are received. All sacramental effects are thus received *ex opere operato*, through the performance of the ritual (literally, by the work worked), and not *ex opere operantis*, through the minister of the sacrament (literally, by the work of the worker). It matters little, therefore, whether a person is baptized by one priest or another, or whether a person goes to one confessor or another; what matters is that the ritual be properly performed, for it is the ritual itself through which the effect is communicated. If the rite is properly performed in all its

---

[21] For a thorough treatment of sacraments and grace within a scholastic context, see Bernard Leeming, S.J., *Principles of Sacramental Theology* (Westminster, Maryland: Newman Press, 1956) chs. 1-3.

essentials, it is said to be valid, and grace is bestowed *ex opere operato*. If the rite is improperly performed, then it is invalid, which is to say it is not a true sacrament at all.[22]

This simple schema, however, is complicated by the fact that grace is not the only effect which results from sacramental rituals. In the Mass, the effect of the words of consecration is the Blessed Sacrament, the Eucharist. Moreover, baptism, confirmation and holy orders cannot be repeated more than one time for the same individual because they are said to confer an indelible character. But neither the Eucharist nor the character is simply a sign (*sacramentum tantum*) or simply the reality (*res tantum*) of grace. In fact, the Eucharist seems to be something of both, for it is both a sign of Christ's presence and the reality of his body and blood. Likewise, the sacramental character is both a sign that one has been baptized, confirmed or ordained, and a supernatural reality that makes one permanently a member of the Church, a confirmed Christian, or a priest. It is therefore both a sign and a reality (*sacramentum et res*), a sacramental reality which is produced by the valid performance of the ritual, either on the altar at Mass, or in the soul of the individual for whom the rite is performed.

Once the theological schema is complete in this way — so that one can speak about the sacramental ritual as a sign (*sacramentum tantum*), the effect of grace as a supernatural reality (*res tantum*), and the other effect as both sign and reality (*sacramentum et res*) — one can legitimately and coherently speak of "administering" and "receiving" sacraments. Note, however, that the sacrament which is administered and received in and through the ritual is the *sacramentum et res*, the sacramental reality. In the Eucharist it is the Blessed Sacrment, given and received in communion. In the three sacraments which can be received only once, it is the sacramental character. In matrimony it is the marriage bond, a sacramental reality which lasts until the death of one of the spouses. In penance and extreme unction

---

[22]On sacramental efficacy and validity, see Leeming, chs. 1 and 8.

the precise sacramental reality is harder to determine (this being one of the details over which the scholastics came to no firm agreement).[23] Viewed thus within the scholastic framework, each sacramental ritual has not one but two effects, the sacramental reality and grace, and this second effect can be further subdivided into sanctifying grace and the particular grace of each sacrament.

If all this sounds rather objective and mechanical, it is partly due to the fact that the Aristotelian-scholastic system was a static one, which could not easily account for variability or individual differences. As an intellectual method it tried to find the unchanging nature of things, or their "essence"; and although it acknowledged the existence of incidental differences, or "accidents," it did not deal with them in any systematic fashion. In sacramental theology, this meant that it sought to determine the essential nature of sacrament in general, and the essence of each of the seven sacraments, but it did not pay attention to the particulars of actual performance, the dynamics of social interaction in the sacraments, or the changes in the rituals over the course of time. It was a static system, which is precisely the type of intellectual system which one would expect to find in the medieval world, which had a stable culture and a stratified society.[24] Nevertheless, the scholastics did recognize that there were, in the administration and reception of the sacraments, certain subjective and personal elements which had to be taken into account.

Regarding the administration of the sacraments, even though the minister does not have to be holy in order to perform a ritual which is an instrumental cause of grace, at the very least he has to have the right intention. That is, he has to intend to perform a valid sacramental action in accordance with the regulations of the Church, which will have the effects ascribed to it in the Church's teachings. Regarding the reception of the sacraments, what is likewise

---

[23]See same, p. 265.
[24]See above, p. 26.

needed is the right intention, which here means the willingness to receive the appropriate sacramental effects. With at least a minimal intention, then, a person can receive the sacramental reality; but to receive the fullest effects of a sacrament, namely all the grace which is offered through it by God, a more positive preparation and receptive disposition is required.[25]

In this way, therefore, scholastic theology attempted to account for the basic objective and subjective elements that medieval Christians were aware of in their sacramental rituals. As already noted, the fundamental soundness of the scholastic approach is attested to by its ability to provide an intellectual foundation for Catholic reflection on the sacraments until well into the twentieth century. At the same time, however, its fundamental weakness was its inflexibility, attested to by its inability to be swayed by Protestant charges of spiritual malaise and popular superstition in sacramental practices, and attested to by its inability to admit the insights of modern philosophies into its system. Thus it was perhaps inevitable that once Catholics themselves began to voice some dissatisfaction with the Tridentine sacraments, and once scriptural and historical studies began to contribute insights which could not easily be handled within scholasticism, Catholic thinkers began to look for alternative ways of understanding and explaining the sacraments.

3. *The Approach of Vatican II*

What is remarkable about the achievement of the Second Vatican Council in calling for a renewal of the Church's sacramental and liturgical life, is that the Catholic bishops did so without appealing to any explicit theology of the sacraments, such as that of scholasticism. In this respect the

---

[25] A rather clear exposition of this aspect of sacramental theology is given in Joseph Pohle and Arthur Preuss, *The Sacraments: A Dogmatic Treatise* (St. Louis, B. Herder, 1943) Vol. I, pp. 161-203.

council fathers were like the early fathers of the Church, who preached and wrote about Christian worship in a pastoral rather than speculative manner, using biblical rather than metaphysical language. The bishops' appeal for reform was therefore based not on philosophical presuppositions but on their own experience of the inner dynamics of worship and their own awareness of the social need for more modern forms of sacramental practice. Recent studies in church history and liturgiology enabled the bishops to see that changes in the past sanctioned the possibility of further changes in the present, and even to perceive the direction that such changes should take. Nevertheless, in the early 1960s the bishops could not foresee the full impact that loosening the bonds of ritual rigidity would have on the Church's liturgical and intellectual life.

What the Second Vatican Council gave the Church, therefore, was not a new theology of the sacraments but a new attitude toward sacramental worship. It was an attitude which was biblical rather than scholastic, and pastoral rather than academic.

The council's biblical attitude toward worship is clearly expressed in the introductory section of the *Constitution on the Sacred Liturgy*:

> Day by day the liturgy builds up those within the Church into the Lord's holy temple, into a spiritual dwelling for God (cf. Eph. 2:21-22) — an enterprise which will continue until Christ's full stature is achieved (cf. Eph. 4:13). At the same time the liturgy marvelously fortifies the faithful in their capacity to preach Christ. To outsiders the liturgy thereby reveals the Church as a sign raised above the nations (cf. Is. 11:12). Under this sign the scattered sons of God are being gathered into one (cf. Jn. 11:52) until there is one fold and one shepherd (cf. Jn. 10:16).[26]

---

[26] Walter M. Abbott, S.J., ed., *The Documents of Vatican II* (London: Geoffrey Chapman, 1966) p. 138.

Especially in the opening paragraphs of Chapter I of the constitution, the council fathers again and again use the language of the scriptures to describe the nature and importance of liturgical worship. For example, they observe that "by baptism, men are plunged into the paschal mystery of Christ: they die with Him, are buried with Him, and rise with Him (cf. Rom. 6:4; Eph. 2:6; Col. 3:1; 2 Tim. 2:11).... In like manner, as often as they eat the supper of the Lord they proclaim the death of the Lord until He comes (cf. 1 Cor. 11:26)."[27] They invoke the image of Christ the high priest developed in the Epistle to the Hebrews, and connect it to the concept of the Church as the body of Christ presented in the letters of St. Paul. "Rightly, then, the liturgy is considered as an exercise of the priestly office of Jesus Christ," which is simultaneously "an action of Christ the priest in His Body the Church."[28] And from this unity of Christians with each other and with their Lord in their worship, especially Eucharistic worship, they conclude that

> the liturgy is the summit toward which the activity of the Church is directed; at the same time it is the fountain from which all her power flows. For the goal of apostolic works is that all who are made sons of God by faith and baptism should come together to praise God in the midst of His Church, to take part in her sacrifice, and to eat the Lord's supper.[29]

Likewise, the bishops' pastoral attitude is evident from the opening lines of the document itself:

> It is the goal of this most sacred Council to intensify the daily growth of Catholics in Christian living; to make more responsive to the requirements of our times those Church observances which are open to adaptation; to nurture whatever can contribute to the unity of all who

---

[27]Same, p. 140.
[28]Same, p. 141.
[29]Same, p. 142.

> believe in Christ; and to strengthen those aspects of the Church which can help summon all of mankind into her embrace.[30]

This pastoral rather than doctrinal perspective is also apparent from the beginning of Chapter III, which is on the sacraments and sacramentals:

> The purpose of the sacraments is to sanctify men, to build up the body of Christ, and finally, to give worship to God. Because they are signs they also instruct. They not only presuppose faith, but by words and objects they also nourish, strengthen, and express it; that is why they are called "sacraments of faith."[31]

Finally, the broadness of the bishops' perspective on the liturgy is clear from the range of issues with which they deal in discussing renewal and reform: attention to liturgical language, vestments and ceremonies; education for both clergy and laity; the importance of liturgical leadership and active participation; the influence of art, architecture and music on worship; the redesign of all of the Church's sacramental rites, with allowances made for regional differences and even individual preferences.

This pastoral attitude toward the sacraments pervades the other conciliar documents as well. In the *Constitution on the Church* (no. 42), Christians are exhorted to grow in the love of God and of one another through prayer and service, through scripture and the sacraments. In the *Decree on the Bishops' Pastoral Office in the Church* (no. 30), pastors are reminded that they should encourage frequent sharing in the sacraments and intelligent participation in the liturgy. And in the *Decree on the Ministry and Life of Priests* (no. 5), the sacraments are described in pastoral terms rather than defined in dogmatic ones: "By baptism men are brought into the People of God. By the sacrament of Penance sinners are reconciled to God and the Church.

---

[30]Same, p. 137.
[31]Same, p. 158.

By the oil of the sick the ailing find relief. And, especially by the celebration of Mass, men offer sacramentally the sacrifice of Christ."[32]

It should also be noted that, despite repeated references to earlier Church documents in footnotes, and despite occasional language reminiscent of doctrinal formulas, the *Constitution on the Sacred Liturgy* makes a strong effort to balance the traditional notion of sacraments as cause of grace with the reminder that they are above all signs of grace: "In the liturgy the sanctification of man is manifested by signs perceptible to the senses, and is effected in a way which is proper to each of these signs."[33] The sacraments "do indeed impart grace, but, in addition, the very act of celebrating them disposes the faithful most effectively to receive grace in a fruitful manner, to worship God duly, and to practice charity."[34] In a similar way the document repeatedly tries to correct the implicit individualism of scholastic sacramental theology by stressing the fact that the liturgical sacraments are communal celebrations, stating that the council "earnestly desires that all the faithful be led to that full, conscious, and active participation in liturgical celebrations which is demanded by the very nature of the liturgy."[35]

In a very real sense, the bishops of the Second Vatican Council did as much for sacramental theology in what they did not say as in what they did say, for they did not speak about the sacraments in traditional scholastic terminology. Without denying the legitimacy of such a conceptual framework for interpreting the nature and function of sacraments in the Christian life, they refused to endorse it as the only possible framework, and they introduced correctives to time-honored imbalances when they did use it. Moreover, by extensively employing the language of the Bible in speak-

---

[32]Same, p. 541. This same descriptive and scriptural language is also found in the more lengthy section on the sacraments in the *Constitution on the Church* (no. 11), pp. 27-29.

[33]Same, p. 141.

[34]Same, p. 158.

[35]Same, p. 144.

ing about the sacraments, they used a language which is fundamental to any theology of the sacraments, and therefore a language which is open to many theological contexts. For the task of sacramental theology is not only to relate liturgical worship to the scriptures and to Christian living, but also to examine it critically and interpret it within a coherent intellectual framework.

4. The Existential/Phenomenological Approach

Next to the scholastic interpretation of the sacraments, the most widespread sacramental theology today is the one developed by Edward Schillebeeckx and Karl Rahner in the fifties and sixties. As already noted, it provided the first philosophical alternative to scholasticism in the modern Church, and it is still the basis of many sacramental theology courses which are taught in Catholic colleges and seminaries.[36]

This approach may be termed existential because it tries to deal with the sacraments concretely rather than abstractly, that is, it seeks to understand what goes on in the

---

[36] The principal work of Schillebeeckx on the sacraments which is available to English speaking readers is *Christ, the Sacrament of the Encounter with God* (New York: Sheed and Ward, 1963). The central ideas in this work are summarized in his article, "The Sacraments: An Encounter with God," *Theology Digest* 7(Spring 1960) pp. 117-121. Other works on the sacraments include *Marriage: Human Reality and Saving Mystery* (New York: Sheed and Ward, 1965), *The Eucharist* (New York: Sheed and Ward, 1968), and *Ministry: Leadership in the Community of Jesus Christ* (New York: Crossroad, 1981).

Karl Rahner's main contribution to sacramental theology first appeared in English as *The Church and the Sacraments* (New York: Herder and Herder, 1963), but many of the ideas it contains are given a more contemporary treatment in Chapter 8 of *Foundations of the Christian Faith* (New York: Seabury Press, 1978). Rahner has also published numerous articles on the sacraments which have been collected in the volumes of his *Theological Investigations* (now published in New York by Crossroad Publishing Company), the principal ones on the general subject of sacraments being: "Concerning the Relationship between Nature and Grace," Vol. I, pp. 297-317; "Personal and Sacramental Piety," Vol. II, pp. 109-133; "Reflections on the Experience of Grace," Vol. III, pp. 86-90; "The Theology of the Symbol," Vol. IV, pp. 221-252; "The Sacramental Basis for the Role of the Layman in the Church," Vol. VIII, pp. 51-74; "The Presence of the

actual celebration of the sacraments and what ac results from participating in sacramental rituals. The approach may also be termed phenomenological because the method it uses to reach this existential understanding is one of attending to the phenomenon of sacramental religion, describing what is revealed in and through religious acts, and providing a theological interpretation of them. It may even be called an experiential approach to the sacraments because the basic phenomena that it attends to are religious experiences, both the personal experiences of individual participants in the sacramental rituals and the social experience of believers whose religious lives are centered on the sacraments. Although the interpretations that Schillebeeckx and Rahner each give to sacramental experience are slightly different, their approaches are similar enough that they may be regarded as using the same basic method in developing their sacramental theology.[37]

Both theologians regard sacraments basically as symbols or symbolic activities, and so underlying their sacramental theory is a philosophical interpretation of symbolism. Understood phenomenologically, any reality that we experience is a symbolic reality in the sense that its outward appearance (the phenomenon) is a sign (a symbol) of what it actually is (its existential being). One can even turn this analysis around and say that "all beings are by their nature symbolic" because they necessarily "express themselves in order to attain their own nature."[38] That is, the existential nature of any being is both embodied in and manifested through something which is a sign of its inner reality. "The symbol strictly speaking (symbolic reality) is the self-

---

Lord in the Christian Community at Worship," Vol. X, pp. 71-83; "What is a Sacrament?" Vol. XIV, pp. 135-148; "Introductory Observations on Thomas Aquinas' Theology of the Sacraments in General," Vol. XIV, pp. 149-160; "Considerations on the Active Role of the Person in the Sacramental Life," Vol. XIV, pp. 161-184. Also helpful is his more popular treatment, *Meditations on the Sacraments* (New York: Seabury Press, 1977).

[37]I have given separate treatment to Schillebeeckx and Rahner in *Doors to the Sacred*, pp. 140-146.

[38]Rahner, *Theological Investigations*, IV, p. 224.

realization of a being in the other, which is constitutive of its essence."³⁹

Although this general analysis applies to all the beings of our experience, its most important application in sacramental theology is to personal beings. For human beings, the body and physical acts incorporate and thus make real what they are as persons and what they are becoming. "The body is not only the manifestation of the human person who reveals himself; it is also the medium in which the soul externalizes its personality development. Thus corporeity becomes a sign of the innermost acts of the person."⁴⁰ For example, people become athletes and scholars, saints and sinners, by choosing to perform different sorts of bodily acts; the result is both that they become incarnations of those various types of persons, and that they reveal what they have become in what they do. Thus, existentially and phenomenologically, any person is a symbolic reality, an incarnate sign of what he or she really is.⁴¹

Moreover, it is only in physical, experienceable activities that persons meet other persons: "The mutual encounter of persons takes place in and through the body."⁴² Therefore, if people are to meet God as a person, the meeting must take place in and through physical signs, that is, symbols or sacraments. "From God's viewpoint, the encounter is revelation; from man's viewpoint, religion. Both revelation and religion then, as the mutual encounter of the created man with the uncreated God, are essentially... sacramental."⁴³ Just as we meet other human beings, reveal ourselves to and

---

³⁹Same, p. 234.

⁴⁰Schillebeeckx in *Theology Digest*, p. 118. See also the almost identical (but philosophically more abstruse) statement by Rahner in "How to Receive a Sacrament and Mean It" in *Theology Digest* 19(Summer 1971) p. 232.

⁴¹For a fuller exposition of this analysis of symbolism and its application to sacramental theology, see John R. Sheets, S.J., "Symbol and Sacrament." *Worship* 41(1967) pp. 194-210; Piet Fransen, S.J., "Sacraments, Signs of Faith," *Intelligent Theology*, Vol. I (Chicago: Franciscan Herald Press, 1969) pp. 126-148.

⁴²Schillebeeckx in *Theology Digest*, p. 118.

⁴³Same, p. 117.

learn about each other through our bodily presence and physical gestures, so also we meet the divine being, embodying our existential attitude toward God in religious acts and discovering what he reveals to us in those same acts. And such acts are sacraments, for they are "a living, personal encounter with God."[44]

In the Christian economy of salvation, however, these individual sacramental acts are secondary, or more precisely, tertiary. The first or primordial sacrament is Jesus Christ, the incarnate Word of God. As Rahner puts it, "the incarnate Word is the absolute symbol of God in the world, filled as nothing else can be with what is symbolized."[45] As Son of the Father, Christ is the Logos, the second person of the Trinity, and as such he is the complete and perfect manifestation of the Godhead within the Godhead itself. But the Logos became flesh in the humanity of Jesus of Nazareth. Therefore, Jesus in his humanity "is the self-disclosure of the Logos itself, so that when God, expressing himself, exteriorizes himself, that very thing appears which we call the humanity of the Logos."[46] Thus, "Christ in his historical existence is both reality and sign...of the redemptive grace of God," which is the inner life of the Trinity.[47]

But Christ as the human externalization of the Trinity was not meant to be a sign of God only to those who lived twenty centuries ago; he is also a revelatory symbol of God for all ages. "The man Jesus, as the personal visible realization of the divine grace of redemption, is *the* sacrament, the primordial sacrament, because this man, the Son of God himself, is intended by the Father to be in his humanity the only way to the actuality of redemption."[48] Jesus was not only the Truth, the true symbol of the Father; he was and

---

[44]Same.
[45]Rahner, *Theological Investigations*, IV, p. 237.
[46]Same, p. 239.
[47]Rahner, *The Church and the Sacraments*, p. 15.
[48]Schillebeeckx, *Christ, the Sacrament*, p. 15.

still is the Way, the means to the Father. "Human encounter with Jesus is therefore the sacrament of the encounter with God."[49] It is in and through Christ that believers meet God and experience the presence and power of his saving grace. "The encounter of the believer with Christ, the primal sacrament (*Ursakrament*) remains the fundamental act of the Christian religion as a personal communion with the three divine Persons."[50]

But where do people encounter Christ, and through Christ come into contact with the saving grace of God? The most important place that this happens is in the Church, the body of Christ, now existent in time and space. "The Church is the abiding presence of that primal sacramental word of definitive grace, which is Christ in the world, effecting what is uttered by uttering it in sign."[51] A second but fundamental sacrament in the Christian economy of salvation is therefore the institutional Church, the Church which was instituted by Christ to continue his work of bringing people into existential contact with God the Father, just as Jesus did. "When we say that the Church is the persisting presence of the incarnate Word in space and time, we imply at once that it continues the symbolic function of the Logos in the world."[52] Thus the Church is the fundamental sacrament, the foundational reality which lies at the basis of all the visible acts of the Church which manifest Christ to the world and open a channel between individuals and God's saving grace. "As the ongoing presence of Jesus Christ in time and space, as the fruit of salvation which can no longer perish, and as the means of salvation by which God offers his salvation to an individual in a tangible way in the historical and social dimension, the church is the basic sacrament."[53]

---

[49] Same.

[50] Schillebeeckx in *Theology Digest*, p. 118.

[51] Rahner, *The Church and the Sacraments*, p. 18. See Schillebeeckx, *Christ, the Sacrament*, p. 41.

[52] Rahner, *Theological Investigations*, IV, p. 240.

[53] Rahner, *Foundations of the Christian Faith*, p. 412.

It is within this context, thirdly, that we can situate the seven ecclesial sacraments (as well as the sacramentals and other "sacraments broadly defined" such as the sacred scriptures[54]). According to Rahner, the sacraments are "acts of the Church, as the basic sacrament of the world's salvation, realizing itself concretely in the life-situation of the individual."[55] In Schillebeeckx's words, "A sacrament, that is an act of the primordial sacrament which is the Church, is a visible action proceeding from the Church as a redemptive institution."[56] Remembering the theory of the symbol which states that the inner nature of any being becomes an existing reality by becoming embodied in something which symbolized its own inner nature, we can say that just as the Word of God came to real existence in our world by becoming incarnate in the person and deeds of Jesus, so also the risen Lord continues his real existence in history by being embodied in the institution and acts of the Church. And the sacraments are essentially acts of the Church. "The sacraments make concrete and actual, for the life of the individual, the symbolic reality of the Church as the primary sacrament and therefore constitute at once, in keeping with the nature of the Church, a symbolic reality."[57]

Looked at from God's side, therefore, "the seven sacraments...are fundamentally an operation of the heavenly Christ that is sacramentalized in the visible, authorized operation of the Church."[58] Looked at from the believer's side, however, the sacraments are occasions for encountering that supernatural operation of the heavenly Christ (another word for which is "grace") within the natural world of human experience.[59] Phenomenologically, then, authen-

---

[54] See Rahner, *Theological Investigations*, IV, p. 221f; XIV, pp. 140, 152.

[55] Rahner in *Theology Digest*, p. 233.

[56] Schillebeeckx, *Christ, the Sacrament*, p. 52.

[57] Rahner, *Theological Investigations*, IV, p. 241.

[58] Schillebeeckx in *Theology Digest*, p. 119.

[59] See Rahner, *Theological Investigations*, III, pp. 86-90; also, Aidan Kavanagh, O.S.B., "Sacrament as an Act of Service," *Worship* 39(1965) pp. 92-94.

tic sacramental celebrations have what Schillebeeckx calls a "dialogue structure," for they are moments of meeting between God and man, they are occasions of interplay between the divine and the human. Existentially understood, "the sacraments are not things, but rather personal, living encounters with the glorified Jesus and, in him, with the living God."[60]

Recently this approach to the sacraments has been extended from the phenomenological realm to the sociological realm by Bernard Cooke. In a series of short articles he develops a sketch for a sacramental theology based on the findings of sociologists that certain types of symbols are "dominant patterns in the imagination that mediate experience and create the world to which we belong," and that they "define the vision of life out of which people operate and thus orient their actions in a certain direction."[61] For when Christians encounter Christ in the sacraments, what they experience is not an undifferentiated sense of the sacred but a meaningful presence of God. Jesus as the Word made flesh in history was a meaningful word uttered by the Father in space and time. This meaning was existentially actualized in Jesus' every human action and definitively symbolized in his death and resurrection. What Jesus did, then, was transform the meaning of human existence by living a new interpretation of what it means to be human; and what the sacraments do is make that transformed meaning, that reinterpretation of what it means to be human, experientially available in the Christian community. Thus when Christians enter into the sacramental celebrations of the Church they enter into a new vision of life by allowing their experience to be restructured into Christ-like patterns of meaning. Ultimately that meaning is the same as the meaning that Jesus experienced in his death and resurrection, but that ultimate meaning is made more concrete for specific human

---

[60]Schillebeeckx in *Theology Digest*, p. 119.

[61]Gregory Baum, *Religion and Alienation* (New York: Paulist Press, 1975) p. 243, p. 242.

situations in the seven ecclesial sacraments. On the one hand, then, living within the Christian community which is the Church transforms the experience of those who accept Christ's death and resurrection as the basic meaning of their lives; and on the other hand, participating in the Church's sacraments effects specific transformations in Christians' experience of birth and maturing, healing and reconciliation, marriage and ministry, and community. And it is precisely such meaningful transformations of human experience which give existential import to what Christians have traditionally termed salvation.[62]

5. *The Process Approach*

Like phenomenology and existentialism, process philosophy began partly as a reaction to traditional modes of thought which placed more emphasis on reality than on our experience of it, and which gave metaphysical priority to being and substance rather than to becoming and change. Process thinkers even contend that traditional philosophies to a large extent reflect the unconscious biases of Western languages which condition us to look at the world and analyze our experience in certain set patterns, and so they often coin new terms in which to present their ideas.[63] This technical vocabulary sometimes makes process philosophy appear esoteric and forbidding to the uninitiated; and though we cannot completely avoid technical terms in presenting a process theology of the sacraments, we can try to

---

[62]See Bernard Cooke, "Understanding the Sacraments Today," a series of articles in *Religion Teacher's Journal*: "The Answer to Life's Basic Questions" (Sept. 1977)39-41; "Jesus Shows Us the Way" (Oct. 1977)31-34; "Community is the Basic Sacrament" (Nov./Dec. 1977)45-48; "Sharing Faith through Baptism and Confirmation" (Jan. 1978)31-33; "The Grace-Giving Reality of Marriage" (Feb. 1978)40-42; "The Power of Healing and Reconciliation" (Mar. 1978)39-41; "The Many Calls to Ministry" (Apr. 1978)37-40; "Eucharist: Sacrament of the Ordinary" (May/June 1978)29-31.

[63]On this point, see Alfred North Whitehead, *Modes of Thought* (New York: Macmillan, 1938), and *Adventures of Ideas* (New York: Macmillan, 1933).

keep as close as possible to ordinary language in a brief exposition such as this one.

Normally when we look at the world, we see things or objects, and we perceive them as being somewhat static or unchanging. Alfred North Whitehead and other process thinkers point out, however, that more basic than the looked at is the looking, more fundamental than the experienced is experience itself. And when we pay attention to our own experiencing we notice at once that it is anything but static; it is always flowing, changing, dynamic. For this reason, Whitehead conceives the nature of experienced reality to be one of continuous process, and he perceives the universe as a vast complex of interacting processes.[64] In other words, process thinking focuses on the flow of continuous becoming; it takes process as primary and regards all beings or entities as events which perdure through time.

Take, for example, human life — and not life in the abstract but life as it is actually experienced. On the one hand, any present moment of our life is what it is because of what we experienced in the past, in both the immediately preceding moment and in the more remote moments through which our life has developed. In a sense, any present occasion grasps or "prehends" past occasions into itself, and by their presence in this moment they cause it to be what it is. But experience is never just a repetiton or composite of the past, and so on the other hand it also includes new possibilities for its future development. That is to say, any occasion also grasps or prehends possible patterns of its own further becoming. Thus on the one hand we are the sum total of our past experiences, but on the other hand we also envisage future possibilities which shape the direction of our personal development.

According to Whitehead, what holds for conscious

---

[64] Whitehead's major exposition of his philosophy is *Process and Reality* (New York: Macmillan, 1929). For introductions to his experiential analysis of reality, see William A. Christian, *An Interpretation of Whitehead's Metaphysics* (New Haven: Yale University Press, 1959); Donald W. Sherburne, *A Key to Whitehead's Process and Reality* (New York: Macmillan, 1966).

human experience is analogously true of all other processes in the universe. The process through which an animal or tree or stone passes, for example, is its own life process or life experience, albeit a process which is not conscious or not as fully conscious as human experience. Any actual occasion in the universe is on the one hand the product of the previous occasions which are related to it and which are prehended by it, and on the other hand it includes within itself an array of future possibilities which it prehends as related to it. Whiteheadian metaphysics, therefore, offers an analysis which holds for all modes of reality. For each of these modes (or what we might commonly think of as types of beings) the process as process is fundamentally the same. What makes them different are simply the elements which enter into the processes in each case. However, since our concern in this section is with process in the human mode, we shall not examine all the details of Whitehead's elaborate metaphysics.[65]

Three elements of that elaborate metaphysical analysis are crucial, nonetheless, for a process understanding of the sacraments: the nature of causality, the social character of reality, and the role God plays in any process of becoming.

As already indicated, causality occurs when any past occasions enter into the internal constitution of an actual occasion, causing it to be what it actually is. By being prehended in an actual occasion, a past occasion becomes actually present within that occasion and thus it is one of its constitutive causes: the actual occasion is the effect of all the other occasions, both major and minor, which it prehends and holds within itself.

From this it can be seen that all reality is essentially social, for all reality involves process, and all process involves prehensions which pull together past occasions into a single actual occasion . That clustering of prehensions in a single moment gives that moment a social character, for it is the

---

[65] A more detailed account of Whitehead's metaphysics, with the nuances needed for a general process theology of the sacraments, is given in Bernard Lee, S.M., *The Becoming of the Church* (New York: Paulist Press, 1974), ch. 2.

composite effect of all the causes which are now present to it.

Finally, it must be recalled that not only past occasions are present in an actual occasion, causing it to be what it is; there is also present a definite array of future possibilities, causing it to be oriented in a certain direction which point the way for its further becoming. But where do those specific possibilities come from? According to Whitehead, they come from God, who is envisaged as that world-embracing actual entity who "completely envisions all potential forms of definiteness, knowing them as pure potential. He, in his primordial nature, maintains the availability of the world's potentiality."[66] That is to say, God is the infinite source of all the forms of definiteness which are available to the entire universe of actual occasions for their future development.

God therefore enters into each and every actual occasion, causing it to be what it is, for what it is is not only the sum of what it prehends out of the past, but also the sum of what it prehends as future possibilities for itself. Moreover, since at every past moment the next moment is only a future possibility, the present moment is always an actualization of possibilities which it had in the past received moment by moment from God. In short, God in a very real way enters into the becoming of all actual occasions, and this is a sort of continuous divine causality.[67]

In the evolving of the physical and biological universe, this divine causality consciously, deliberately and lovingly guides the becoming of each and every actual occasion from what it is to what it may yet be.

> The world is a process of creative advance. At each moment reality is called to become more than it was before — and the issuing of this summons is one of the

---

[66]Lee, p. 66.

[67]For a fuller picture of the process portrayal of God, see Charles Hartshone, *The Divine Relativity* (New Haven: Yale University Press, 1948), and *A Natural Theology for Our Time* (LaSalle, Illinois: Open Court, 1967); also W. Norman Pittenger, *God in Process* (London: SCM Press, 1967), and John B. Cobb, *God and the World* (Philadelphia: Westminster Press, 1969).

functions of God in the world. He is a call to transcendence.[68]

God is thus present in every act of becoming, suggesting the ways that it may become its best self and even go beyond itself, taking into consideration what it has already become and the environment through which it will progress, both of which impose limitations on its becoming.

In the evolving of the human universe, however, a new dimension is added, and this is the dimension of consciousness and deliberate choice on the part of individuals and societies. Future human possibilities are offered to persons through acts of imagination which envision alternative courses of action. Because of this element of choice, therefore, persons can accept or reject divinely offered possibilities of becoming. In traditional theological language, they can cooperate with God's grace, or they can sin.

Theoretically, then, if a person kept himself radically open to God's call and responded to it completely at each and every moment of his existence, every occasion in that person's life would be filled with God's presence. Such a life would be one of total fidelity to God's grace. In addition, such fidelity would be cumulative since each new moment of such a life would already contain a strong presence of God conditioning and guiding this person's additional possibilities of becoming. Christianity contends, however, that this description is more than a mere theoretical possibility; it has already been realized in the personal life of Jesus of Nazareth:

> The cumulative fidelity of Jesus to the call of God is a way of explaining the extraordinary presence of God in and to Jesus. Such fidelity could only be achieved with extraordinary awareness and deliberate human choices, that is, with consciousness of God's immediacy to one's acts of becoming. And that is part of the claim of Jesus: the

[68]Lee, p. 204.

centrality and immediacy of God's presence in his very existence and his awareness of the fact.[69]

Jesus' moment by moment experience was therefore completely penetrated by both human and divine prehensions. On every occasion of his life he prehended both what he had humanly become as well as the divine possibilities of his further becoming. The resultant form or structure of Jesus' life experience was at once both completely human and completely divine, and since experience is but another way of talking about process or existence, we can say that the structure of Jesus' existence was both human and divine. In more traditional language, Jesus was both man and God.

Jesus' life in human history, however, had a beginning and an end, and so we can speak of that historical trajectory of Jesus occasions collectively as the Jesus event. As past, it was completed, but as completed the Jesus event (and individual occasions which comprised it) is now eternally available to be prehended as an element in the becoming of all other human occasions. This was of course true in a direct and immediate way for those who saw and heard the man Jesus in his life time, for his actions and words displayed the shape of this human/divine existence. But this is also true in a less direct way for Christians today who see and hear the deeds and sayings of Jesus in the scriptures, in sermons, in the liturgy and in other events that mediate the life of Jesus to them. In both the immediate and mediated ways, however, the forms of definiteness which comprise the Jesus event are symbolic forms, that is, they are structures or signs of past occasions which have the same structure as those events themselves. "The symbols which enable consciousness to see the penetration of the past into the present are detachable, that is, symbols can be elicited even when the event to which they refer is no longer spatially or temporally

---

[69]Same, p. 115. For a fuller presentation of process Christology, see John B. Cobb, *The Structure of Christian Existence* (Philadelphia: Westminster Press, 1967); W. Norman Pittenger, *The Word Incarnate* (New York: Harper and Brothers, 1959) and *Christology Reconsidered* (London: SCM Press, 1970).

close. Yet through those symbols, the past can continue to invade the present since the symbols do indeed participate in the past."[70]

Furthermore, symbols have two important features in the way that they make past events available to present experience. The first is: "Symbols simplify the data. They single out certain characteristics through which an event is experienced."[71] The written gospels, for example, are not complete chronologies of the life of Jesus but rather they are symbolic representations of significant occasions in the Jesus event through which that event can be perceived and felt as present here and now. The second is: "Because symbols determine how we get hold of a past event, they influence the shape of new events."[72] That is, symbols in their functioning as symbols communicate certain characteristics of a past event into present thought and action. By meditating on the gospels, for example, Christians allow the forms of definiteness present in the Jesus event to penetrate into their own consciousness and shape their own experience:

> The Jesus event is important to life. That means that the Christian attempts to bring that event into frequent contact with his life and the Church's life. The Jesus event and history engage each other in the ongoingness of daily routine.
>
> *Being* a Christian is a result of a constant kind of *experiencing* which makes the Jesus event play a constitutive role in one's own becoming.[73]

In the ordinary way of talking about things we say that Jesus had a group of disciples who formed the first Christian community and that this was the beginning of the Church.

---

[70]Lee, p. 105f. For Whitehead's elaboration of this theory, see his *Symbolism: Its Meaning and Effect* (New York: Macmillan, 1927).

[71]Lee, p. 107.

[72]Same.

[73]Same, p. 172.

In process terminology we would say instead that the process begun in the Jesus event was prehended by subsequent actual occasions and became a defining characteristic of their life trajectories. Although each Christian did this individually, they also did this close to and with the help of other persons who were doing the same in their own process of becoming Christian. Thus they formed what in Whiteheadian terms is technically called a society or nexus, a cluster of actual occasions occurring in spatial and temporal proximity, and joined together by their prehensions of one another. Since they each prehend forms of definiteness from the Jesus event and embody them in their own becoming, when they prehend one another, the defining characteristics of the Jesus event become embodied by the society and become its own defining characteristics as well. Thus the Jesus life of the Christian community is transmitted through human history not merely by individuals reading the gospels, for example, but also by individuals living together and learning how to be Christian from one another.

Although a number of contemporary theologians (mostly Protestant) have used process philosophy as the framework for their thinking,[74] only one has thus far used process categories to develop a full ecclesiology and sacramental theology. In *The Becoming of the Church* (already cited a number of times in this section) Bernard Lee describes the Christian community as a society in a strict Whiteheadian sense. As indicated in the previous paragraph, such a society is not so much an aggregate of individuals (in the non-Whiteheadian sense) as an ongoing intersection of personal processes, each separately and all together characterized by those same forms of definiteness which characterized the Jesus event. As Lee never tires of reminding us, in Whiteheadian metaphysics, "*process itself is the reality*. Thus too,

---

[74]See, for example, Robert B. Mellert, *What is Process Theology?* (New York: Paulist Press, 1975), and Marjorie Hewitt Suchocki, *God Christ Church: A Practical Guide to Process Theology* (New York: Crossroad, 1982). Helpful are the anthologies, Delwin Brown, Ralph James and Gene Reeves, eds., *Process Philosophy and Christian Thought* (Indianapolis: Bobbs Merril, 1971), and Ewert Cousins, ed., *Process Theology: Basic Writings* (New York: Newman Press, 1971)

the Church's becoming is its reality."[75] That is, the Church is "an event whose process is its reality."[76] Seen from this perspective, the Church is neither an institution nor an organization nor even a community, if by community one means a collection of individuals. Rather, the Church is an ongoing collective activity, and so where that activity is, there is the Church, and where that activity is not, the Church is absent. And what is that activity? Lee specifies it in some detail, but in general we can say that it is activity which has the same forms of definiteness as the Jesus event:

> The Church believes in the importance of Jesus; Christians...intend to let their lives be shaped by the inclusion of the Jesus event as an occasion of their experience. It is principally in the life of the Church that the Jesus event continues its presence, and it is from and in the Church that men hear of it and learn to let their lives be touched by it. Lives-being-touched-by-Jesus is the process which constitutes the actuality of the Church."[77]

The ways that Christians let the human/divine activity of the Jesus event invade their lives are manifold, but they are primarily symbolic: scripture, preaching, music, art, etc. For fifteen centuries all of Christianity, however, and since then the Catholic and Orthodox churches have insisted on the importance of sacramental ritual for becoming Christian. "The Sacramental life of the Church is the main dynamic through which the Jesus event continues to take hold of the lives of men. Through the Sacraments the Church is creative of the Christian and the Christian is creative of the Church."[78] On the one hand, the sacraments are social rituals, for they all involve communal action in which the forms of definiteness which define the Christian mode of existence are both enacted and experienced by all

---

[75] Lee, p. 172.
[76] Same, p. 206.
[77] Same, p. 205.
[78] Same.

who participate in the rituals. On the other hand, the sacraments are symbolic rituals, for they make what is past available in the present: "A Sacrament is a positive prehension of the Jesus event. The Jesus event is felt *there* and made to be *here*."[79] Moreover, just as each of the gospel stories does not depict the entire Jesus event, so also the seven individual sacraments symbolize specific aspects of that event and make it present here and now. "Not only does each of the Sacraments objectify the Jesus event from a definite perspective, but each of them has the possibility of adding further specification as the Jesus event is related to the particularities of a person or situation of a community."[80]

Understood in this way, the sacraments also have the causal efficacy that Christian doctrine has always claimed for them, but the causality of the sacraments is interpreted differently within the Whiteheadian framework. For process thinkers, causality occurs whenever one actual occasion is present to another, entering into its internal constitution and making it to be what it is. And since the sacraments make occasions of the Jesus event present in the experiential life of Christians, they can be said in Whiteheadian terms to be causally efficacious.

Still, such an efficaciousness is not automatic. Because sacraments are only symbols of the Jesus event there is no *a priori* guarantee that their forms of definiteness will always reflect the structure of the event that they are supposed to symbolize; both the abstract rites themselves and their actual enactment must have a shape through which occasions in the Jesus event can be perceived and prehended. And in addition, the contemporary occasions for which the Jesus occasions are available must be open to receiving them, that is, their forms of definiteness must already be somewhat similar to the forms of definiteness which they are to receive from the Jesus event. Thus Lee insists that "the

[79] Same, p. 212.
[80] Same, p. 181.

Sacramental symbols must *in fact* participate in both the Jesus event and contemporary possibilities for the Sacrament to do its work. For a symbol actualizes what it symbolizes in the Sacrament, and the symbol must have a real basis."[81] That is to say, in order for a sacrament to actualize what it symbolizes, what it is to actualize in the life of the individual or the community must to some extent be already there, ready to be actualized in the sacramental moment.

> Baptism, for example, is doomed to be ineffectual if the one baptized is not really introduced into a community where Christian love is operative. To be baptized is to be received into the Church. But the Church is not a place or thing. The actuality of the Church is in process.... Where there is not that process, there is not the actuality of the Church; there is no event into which one can enter.[82]

A process theology of the Sacraments can therefore be critical as well as explanatory. It is not simply an explanation of how sacraments work when they work, which is to say, when they are effective signs of God's inner life; but it also offers a basis for a critique of sacramental performance, showing why liturgical rituals do not always have the effects that they are supposed to have.

Perhaps the best summary of Lee's sacramental theology can be given in his own words:

> Christian faith believes that in Jesus there is a revelation par excellence of the love of God and the design (Logos) of God. The events of the life and death of Jesus show a configuration of human life responding fully to the summons of God. God touched history very powerfully in Jesus, and he continues the presence of that special appearance in the appropriation of the Jesus event in the life of the Church. The Church, because it presents God to the world over and over again through a constant

---

[81]Same, p. 244.
[82]Same, p. 218f.

reappropriation of the Jesus event, is a reflection of God at work in the world....

Christianity is a call to a personhood that is shaped by a way of loving. That call is above all exercised in and through Christian community, that is Church. And again it is the Sacramental structure of the Church's life which is a principal means of expressing that call and responding to it.[83]

6. The Charismatic Approach

In 1967 a small group of Catholics in Pittsburgh, Pennsylvania, underwent a religious experience which transformed their lives and since then has affected the lives of thousands more.[84] It was the sort of religious experience that had been associated mainly with classical Protestant pentecostalism, but after overcoming their astonishment about what had happened to them they began to discover that there were precedents for such happenings described in a number of New Testament passages. It would appear that something similar had happened to Jesus' disciples on the feast of Pentecost, and that such behavior was not unknown in some of the earliest Christian communities. Because the things that happened to people in the midst of such experiences appeared to be God-given graces or charisms (the Greek word for grace is *charis*), those who received these spiritual gifts — speaking in tongues, making prophetic statements, healing emotional or physical illness, a strong and inspiring faith in God, and the like — became known as charismatic Christians, and the spiritual revival which swept through the Roman Catholic and other churches came to be called the charismatic renewal.

Initially, Catholics who became part of this movement

---

[83]Same, p. 204f, p. 183.

[84]See Kevin and Dorothy Ranaghan, *Catholic Pentecostals* (New York: Paulist Press, 1969) ch. 1.

joined loosely organized groups that ranged in size from a few members to a few hundred, meeting perhaps once or twice a week for prayer and Bible study, besides attending Sunday Mass in their regular parish. For many Catholic charismatics this is still the way that they arrange their religious involvements, but in the mid-1970s some of them began experimenting with communal living situations patterned on the sharing of lives and goods that they saw exemplified in the New Testament communities.[85] This closer and continuous charismatic living, as well as increasing contact between pentecostal Catholics at meetings, retreats and conventions, engendered a good deal of theological reflection on the nature and purpose of charismatic communities in the Church.[86] And the participation of priests as well as laity and religious in Eucharistic and other sacramental celebrations inevitably led to a reflection on the specifically charismatic experience of sacraments.[87] Not without justification, many Catholics in the movement believe that early Christianity was largely a collection of charismatic communities and that the most authentic form of Christian worship is charismatic in nature.[88] For this reason, even though a charismatic theology of the sacraments arises out of the experience of sacramental worship in one style of Catholicism, the claim that charismatic faith is normative for all Christianity gives such a theology a potentially more universal significance. Michael Scanlan and Ann Thérèse Shields, for instance, use the metaphor of encountering Christ to describe what happens in all the

[85] See Acts 2:42-47; 4:32-37.

[86] See Donald Gelpi, S.J., *Pentecostalism: A Theological Viewpoint* (New York: Paulist Press, 1971); Kilian McDonnell, O.S.B., *Charismatic Renewal and the Churches* (New York: Seabury Press, 1970).

[87] See especially Michael Scanlan, T.O.R. and Ann Thérèse Shields, R.S.M., *And Their Eyes Were Opened* (Ann Arbor, Michigan: Servant Books, 1976); Donald L. Gelpi, S.J., *Charism and Sacrament* (New York: Paulist Press, 1976).

[88] For example, Gelpi asserts: "The only community in which the eucharist can be authentically celebrated is, therefore, a charismatic community.... By the same token, sound liturgical renewal is possible only through the integration of charismatic and sacramental worship." *Charism and Sacrament*, p. 232.

Catholic sacraments, and this way of speaking about the sacraments is already accepted by many non-charismatic theologians. Similarly, Donald Gelpi uses the language of process theology, which is not charismatic in origin, to explain what is and should be happening in any sacramental experience, not only the experience of charismatic Christians.

Although it is implicit in all charismatic treatments of prayer and worship, Gelpi lays the foundation for his own sacramental theology explicitly on the phenomenon of conversion. He insists, moreover, that an adequate understanding of sacramental worship presupposes not only Christian conversion but also affective, moral and intellectual conversion. For true conversion is not just a change in beliefs but an entire transformation of the way a person feels and behaves, thinks and makes decisions. Basically it involves a reorientation of one's whole experiential life from passively allowing it to be shaped by the past to actively shaping it in response to creative possibilities offered by God.[89]

Even prior to our conversion (as well as during and after it), God through his Spirit is calling us forward to human maturity and Christ-like existence. It is the invitation of grace which is always and everywhere at work in the world, and which we might dimly sense in our feelings or imagination as a movement towards a nameless fulfillment or even just to an escape from our present emptiness. Then, if we assent to that impulse and allow it to guide us, we find ourselves being inwardly touched and shaped by what we later come to recognize as the Spirit of God. "Sometimes the touches of the Spirit are only vaguely felt: they enter prayer in an undefined sense of peace and divine presence. At times his touch is clearer and breeds visions, insights, words, new understanding."[90] The Spirit affects our thinking, giving us what was traditionally called the grace of faith, leading us to trust God, opening us to an understnding of his revelation in the scriptures, in our religious heritage and in the world

---

[89] See Gelpi, same, chs. 1 and 2.
[90] Same, p. 14.

around us. He affects our feelings, calling us to repentance, softening our stubbornness, healing our distorted emotions. And he affects our behavior, moving us to act without self-interest, prompting us to creatively change the world, suggesting that we share what we have with others. For ultimately conversion affects every aspect of our personal and social life. "The integrally converted Christian is one who stands in complete openness to every impulse of the Spirit of God."[91]

Normally for the Christian, however, both the call to conversion and the energy needed to sustain it come in and through the community of believers, the Church. "We perceive the Spirit of Jesus inferentially in the words and deeds of persons who believe in Christ and whose lives are open to the transforming presence of His Spirit."[92] Thus the grace of conversion is an invitation to holiness, to become like Jesus, "to allow the Spirit to shape one's mind to the mind of Christ."[93] The ability to actually do that, moreover, is not something that comes from ourselves but from God, through the experienced power of his Spirit working within us. It is therefore a gift, a grace, a charism of personal sanctification — or more accurately, it is a variety of charisms or graces which have sometimes been called the seven gifts of the Holy Spirit. Those who allow themselves to be thus led by the Spirit can properly be called charismatic Christians, and together with other such Christians they form a truly charismatic community.

But the gifts of personal sanctification are not the only ones that God offers to those who are willing to be led by the Spirit. In a letter to the Corinthians, St. Paul mentions a variety of charisms that are given to Christians for the service of the community, and in other letters he speaks of various ministries or calls to service within the Church.[94]

---

[91] Same, p. 15.
[92] Same, p. 14.
[93] Same, p. 29.
[94] See I Cor. 12:8-10, 28-31; Rom. 12:6-8.

Paul insists that these particular gifts are given not for the benefit of the individuals who have them but for "the building up of the body of Christ," which is the Church, or more specifically, the local church community. Those who find that they have the charism of preaching, giving instruction, speaking words of prophesy, healing physical or spiritual illness, praising God in strange tongues, performing works of mercy, leading people, administering programs, and so on, are — by the very fact that they have been given these gifts — called by the Spirit to use them in the service of others. These gifts are therefore not charisms of personal sanctification but charisms of service to the community.

Now, if sacrament is, broadly and simply, "a sign of a sacred reality," or "an outward sign of an inward grace," then all charisms which are active in a Christian community are sacramental in two ways. They are "expressively sacramental" in that they externalize gifts which have been received from God, giving them concrete shape in the personal lives of individuals and the communal life of the Church. But they are also "interpretatively sacramental" since those who have faith can perceive them as manifestations of the Father's love, continuations of Christ's work, and revelations of the Spirit's power in the world. Ideally, any such charismatic actions in the experience of Christians are sacramental in both ways:

> Experience takes on primordial sacramentality when expressive and interpretative sacramentality fuse within the same experience, when an event of grace is perceived in faith to be such and evokes the proper graced response.[95]

The "proper graced response" is first of all a worshipful and thankful acknowledgment of God present and working in our midst. This is true of all such sacramental occasions. But secondly there is a distinct response that is called forth by each distinctly different manifestation of a sacramental

[95] Gelpi, Same, p. 107.

charism: an increase in Christian unity, a desire to serve others, a willingness to extend Christ's lordship over more areas of our life, a healing of past grievances, a deeper understanding of God's word in the scriptures, and so on. And all of these sacramental moments in the individual and communal experience of Christians lead ultimately to the building up of the body, to their becoming a community of persons who are fundamentally a sacramental sign to themselves and to the world of God's grace at work in human history, because they are becoming inwardly and outwardly changed by that grace. To put it briefly, "the charisms of sanctification and of service are integral to the Church's primordial sacramentality precisely because they mediate the conscious transformation of the Christian community in faith."[96]

For Gelpi and for other charismatic Christians, it is only in a Christian community which exhibits and recognizes the full range of charismatic gifts that the Gospel message of salvation in Christ makes full, experientially verifiable, self-authenticating, sense.

> It is through the sharing of all the gifts, from the gifts of sanctification to the gift of tongues, that the Christian community comes to experience itself consciously and concretely as redeemed. For it is in the course of such sharing that it comes to recognize itself as God's own people, those whom God has claimed in love for himself through the transforming power of his Spirit.[97]

But Gelpi is also a Catholic Christian and he acknowledges that in the historical experience of the Church seven potentially charismatic moments have become designated as "sacramental" in a more specific sense than the broad sacramental meaning that can be attributed to any manifestation of God's grace. These are the seven ecclesial sacraments in the life of the universal Church as a worshipping

---

[96]Same, p. 107f.
[97]Same, p. 240. See also Scanlan and Shields, pp. 15-18.

community (as contrasted with the local community or prayer group which may also cherish its own peculiar rituals that are sacramental for it). Reflecting on his (and other Catholics') charismatic experience of these official church rituals, he offers a general "descriptive definition" of a sacrament properly so called:

> A sacrament is an act of new covenant worship which, through the presence of an authorized minister, engages the faith of the Church universal by challenging the recipient of the sacrament kerygmatically and prophetically to an appropriate response in faith to the graces ritually proclaimed and sought from God in the name of Jesus and in the power of his Spirit.[98]

Scanlan and Shields offer a similar but somewhat looser definition of an ecclesial sacrament:

> A sacrament is a visible sign of God's desire and pledge to deepen his relationship with us. It promises the gifts of grace we seek: healing, nourishing, cleansing, freeing, consecrating, blessing, empowering us to accept his reign in our lives and deepening our covenant with him and his people.[99]

To accurately understand either "charismatic definition" of the Church's sacraments, however, it is crucial to keep in mind the particularly charismatic experience of the sacraments out of which they arise, which they therefore in some way "describe," and in reference to which they make sense. But if the intuition of Catholic pentecostals is correct, namely that the early Church was basically a charismatic community, and if the claim that follows from this is also correct, namely that the Church today should be at bottom a charismatic community, then what Gelpi and others say

---

[98] Gelpi, same, p. 138. For a fuller exposition of this definition, see p. 113f.

[99] Scanlan and Shields, p. 38. For their application of this definition to each of the seven sacraments, see pp. 10-12.

about the sacraments becomes important for the entire Church.

Granted, then, that the seven ecclesial sacraments are ritual signs specifically designated to express the faith of the whole Church, to prophetically proclaim the universal dimensions of God's grace, and to be presided over by an authorized minister, the inner workings of these seven still exhibit the same charismatic structure shown in the manifestation of any of the more broadly sacramental charismatic gifts, as already described.

Thus in baptism, the charismatically Christian community makes the grace of redeemed living concretely available to newcomers, whether adults or infants, through the traditional signs of washing with water and profession of faith, for in that ritual action it pledges itself to be faithful to its covenant with God, with each other and with the newcomer, and it thereby re-actualizes the conditions which make salvation possible. Likewise in confirmation, the leader of the local church calls each candidate to full Christian conversion and service to the community, and "the sacramental worshipper professes personal willingness to be transformed visibly by the Spirit as the apostles were transformed on Pentecost."[100] In the rituals of marriage and ordination that general Christian call to service is made more specific, for the community in these sacramental ceremonies proclaims either that it has discerned a charism of covenant fidelity and atoning love that two Christians have for one another, and which will lead to the building up of the body, or that it has discerned a charism of self-sacrificing ministry and spirit-filled leadership, which will meet the pastoral and liturgical needs of the church. In penance and the anointing of the sick, the words and gestures of the priest bring the healing power of the Spirit into contact with the felt need of Christians to be loosed from the bondage of sin and sickness, and to be freed to respond in love to God and others despite their past moral failings or

---

[100]Gelpi, Same, p. 146.

their present physical debility. Finally, the Eucharist "is the act of the Christian community as such, assembled in faith to proclaim before God and one another the divine saving action that binds them together as a community."[101] That saving action is Christ's death and resurrection, and to the extent that Christians consciously enter into that action in their worship, thanking God for having made it available to them, and through participation in the ritual experiencing a death to self-reliance and a rebirth in willing obedience to the Father in the power of the Spirit, to that extent they cooperate in making present the mystery of Christ that both saves the world and makes them a charismatic community.[102]

In a charismatic approach to the sacraments, then, any liturgical ritual "demands a personal commitment of faith that engages one totally."[103] It is only when a sacramental event "is immanent to a worshipper's experience" that it "shapes it efficaciously."[104] Without the foundation of authentic conversion and the actually present receptivity of the Spirit, not even an ecclesial sacrament can have a charismatic effect. But on the other hand, "when the sacramental worshipper is properly disposed, the sacramental act does ... contain and effects the very pneumatic transformation it signifies."[105] Or to say it slightly differently,

> The depth of the encounter with Jesus depends on how deeply we enter the covenant [to which we are called as Christians]. The more completely we give ourselves to live as God's people under the leadership of Jesus, the more meaningful is the encounter.[106]

---

[101]Same, p. 229.
[102]See also Scanlan and Shields, pp. 10-12.
[103]Gelpi, same, p. 115.
[104]Same.
[105]Same, p. 135.
[106]Scanlan and Shields, p. 35 (parenthesis added).

7. The Liberation Approach

Around the same time that Catholic pentecostalism was beginning in North America, a new style of theology was beginning in South America. But whereas charismatic Christianity focused primarily on the conversion of the individual and his or her relation to God, liberation theology has been mainly concerned with the transformation of the Church and its relation to society. For the pentecostal movement began among people whose principal anxiety was spiritual apathy in a nation of middle class affluence, but the liberation movement was begun by people who felt the need to react against the exploitation of the poor in oppressive military dictatorships.

The need for a radically new style of Catholic theology was first felt by theologians who saw that for the most part the Church in Latin America had identified itself with the ruling class, the "power elites" in their countries, and that it had for a long time done little to alleviate the misery of the rural peasants and the urban poor, the "powerless masses" who constituted perhaps nine-tenths of the population. They sensed that the situation of these Christians was not unlike that of the Israelites enslaved in Egypt, and they saw that the Jesus of the gospels was primarily concerned with the weak and the poor; and yet traditional theology seemed to tell people to accept their suffering and wait patiently for heaven. Moreover, these (mostly young) theologians had learned from sociology and political philosophy (especially Marxism) that the symbolic images which people accept as the basic structures of reality largely determine the way they think and react to the world around them.[107] Thus these theologians saw a need to rebuild Christian theology from the ground up, to begin with their intuition that any authentic theology had to be concerned about the oppressed, and that the images that it presents of God, Church, salvation

---

[107]See pp. 55-56 and 134 above.

and so on must enable people to recognize and liberate themselves from oppression.[108]

Among the theologians who are thus attempting to rethink the meaning of Christianity in the light of their politically oppressive social situation, only Juan Luis Segundo has dealt extensively with the nature and purpose of the Church's sacraments.[109] Segundo believes that for centuries the sacraments in the Latin American Church (and by extension, the rest of the Church) have been for all practical purposes magical rites and instruments of political oppression. What they ought to be, however, are consciousness-raising signs of ecclesial responsibility and vehicles for social liberation. He therefore proposes that the old magical theology of the sacraments should be discarded in favor of a new and more critical sacramental theology.[110] To appreciate how Segundo arrives at this radical conclusion, however, we need first to look at some of his theological premises.

Like many other liberation theologians, Segundo contends that authentic Christianity is "this-worldly" and not "other-worldly." For untold millennia, religion assumed that

---

[108] For background and an introduction to liberation theology, see Hugo Latorre Cabal, *The Revolution of the Latin American Church* (Norman, Oklahoma: University of Oklahoma Press, 1978); Thomas M. McFadden, ed., *Liberation, Revolution, and Freedom* (New York: Seabury Press, 1975); Rosemary Reuther, *Liberation Theology* (New York: Paulist Press, 1972). For some basic writings by liberation theologians themselves, see Gustavo Gutierrez, *A Theology of Liberation* (Maryknoll, New York: Orbis Books, 1973); Leonardo Boff, *Liberating Grace* (Maryknoll, New York: Orbis Books, 1979); Jon Sobrino, S.J., *Christology at the Crossroads*, (Maryknoll, New York: Orbis Books, 1978).

[109] See Juan Luis Segundo, S.J., *A Theology for Artisans of a New Humanity* (Maryknoll, New York: Orbis Books): Vol. I, *The Community Called Church* (1973); Vol. II, *Grace and the Human Condition* (1973); Vol. III, *Our Idea of God* (1973); Vol. IV, *The Sacraments Today* (1974); Vol. V, *Evolution and Guilt* (1974). For his understanding of the task of theology today, see *The Liberation of Theology* (Maryknoll, New York: Orbis Books, 1976). For a comprehensive introduction to Segundo's work, see Alfred T. Hennelly, *Theologies in Conflict* (Maryknoll, New York; Orbis Books, 1979).

[110] For a summary of these points, see Hennelly, pp. 96-98; Segundo, *The Liberation of Theology*, pp. 40-43. Segundo is of course thinking primarily of scholastic sacramental theology and the sort of sacramental ritualism which it is sometimes used to justify.

the sacred was separate from the profane, that the gods lived in a world outside history. Along with this, religious morality was fundamentally a reflection of the existing social order, and so myth and ritual taught people to accept that order as sacred and to conform their behavior to it. Even ancient Judaism, he believes, did not free itself entirely from this religious mentality, for it still saw God as utterly transcendent and morality as an unimaginative conformity to the divine will.[111] With the coming of Christ, however, this outlook was exactly reversed. God's revelation in Jesus is that the transcendent reality is radically immanent in human history, and the good news of the Gospel is that people have the God-given power to love one another creatively in shaping their own destiny. Thus grace is simply "God himself made into our existence"; it is the human spirit, "the Spirit that dwells in us."[112] Seen in this light, salvation is a work of liberation, a work of people freeing themselves with God's help from domination by physical, psychological and social forces. "God has no plan for us except to associate us with his creative work in the history of the universe."[113] But this implies that Christianity is fundamentally secular rather than religious in the traditional sense of the word. "At bottom secularization means that everything in the Church, absolutely everything, must be translated from 'religious' terms into man's task in history."[114]

But what about Jesus? Didn't Christ come to establish a new religion and to give human beings the sacraments as a means of salvation? No, says Segundo, if by religion you mean the worship of a transcendent God outside history, and if by sacraments you mean cultic rituals by means of

---

[111] Many scripture scholars and contemporary theologians, it should be noted, would not agree with this. It seems that on this point Segundo's use of the Old Testament is rather one-sided. Of course there are also other theologians who would disagree with him on other points as well.

[112] Segundo, *Grace and the Human Condition*, p. 169.

[113] Same, p. 169f. See also pp. 30-35.

[114] Segundo, *Our Idea of God*, p. 78.

which individuals can get to heaven. Although one can find isolated texts in the scriptures to prove that the Church should have religious rituals, "a complete reading of the New Testament does not suggest, at first glance, that Jesus meant to establish any sacred rites — in the strict sense of the term."[115] Religious rites before the time of Christ were strictly magical, for magic in primitive and other religions is intrinsically an attempt to produce supernatural effects through human actions.[116] Furthermore, "one of the essential elements of the gospel seems to be that the community formed to succeed Jesus is not going to have sacred rites, gestures or words endowed with divine power. In short it is not going to have magic signs that lead people to salvation."[117] On the contrary, Segundo's "complete reading of the New Testament" forces him to conclude that "the overall context indicates that man's whole destiny depends on just and cordial relations with his neighbor. This is so true that the necessity of righting these relations takes precedence over strictly religious functions."[118] Arguing from Hebrews 10, which describes how Christ's unique priesthood did away with the need for temple sacrifice, Segundo reasons that "human beings, then, no longer need sacred intermediaries or sacred mediations."[119] And he analyzes John 6, Ephesians 2, and Colossians 1 and 2 to show that the commonly accepted interpretation of these passages is mistaken: salvation does not come through faith *and* baptism but through faith *or* baptism, for Christian baptism intrinsically assumes the presence of active faith; and so it is always faith, not the

---

[115] Segundo, *The Sacraments Today*, p. 22.

[116] "Magic, reduced to its essential elements, consists of the quest for an efficacy that goes beyond man's powers. It achieves this by recourse to superior powers, whom it tries to get to operate in a specific way through symbolic gestures. These gestures, taking on superhuman power but nevertheless controlled by man through symbolism, will produce the proper effect directly." Segundo, *The Community Called Church*, p. 37f.

[117] Segundo, *The Sacraments Today*, p. 22.

[118] Same. To support this contention, he cites Mt. 5:21-24, and Jn. 4:20-24.

[119] Same, p. 23.

ritual of immersion in water, that effects the saving transformation of people's lives.[120]

This does not deny the fact that Jesus used the common ritual gestures of his culture and that some of these (such as sharing a meal of fellowship) were picked up and repeated by his followers. But it does deny that these gestures were intended by Jesus or experienced by his followers as anything more than communal signs of social realities. "So far as we know, the Christian living in the primitive Church saw these distinctive signs of his community" not as "something useful or even necessary for eternal life" but as "spontaneous gestures in a community that was [already] in possession of eternal life."[121] What today we call sacraments were at that time ritual expressions of things that were really happening in the Christian community: the sharing of life and goods, the alleviation of physical and emotional suffering, the welcoming of newcomers into a redeemed life through faith in Jesus, the reconciliation of people with one another, the designation of certain individuals to particular tasks in the Church, and so on. On the one hand, these communal gestures were consciousness-raising signs through which Christians become aware of what God through his Spirit was doing in human history, and especially in their own lives. But on the other hand, they were also efficacious signs because they made grace tangibly available to the Church in its mission of transforming human society, of bringing about God's kingdom on earth.

With the wholesale adoption of Christianity as the religion of the Roman Empire, however, people brought into the Church those very same "religious" attitudes which Jesus had deliberately rejected. "In passing from a Christian practice rooted in conversion, in which God's revelation appealed to liberty, to a mass Christianity, the formulas of faith and ritual formulas tended to be simplified and made

---

[120]See same, p. 25f. Along these lines, he notes on p. 44 that in I Cor. 1:11-17, "Paul himself had to fight against the notion that baptism had an almost automatic religious effectiveness."

[121]Same, p. 42 (parenthesis added).

more immediate."[122] That is, salvation was thought to result immediately from saying the right words and performing the proper rituals. And this, in essence, is magic. The mass baptism of barbarians during the Dark Ages only perpetuated the magical attitude in the Church. Theologians in the Middle Ages and afterwards uncritically supposed that this attitude was proper to Christianity, and so they tried to differentiate Catholic rituals from pagan ones on the basis of efficacy, claiming that the Christian rites are "the only efficacious ones. The other rites deceive people; their effect is not truly achieved."[123] In fact, however, Christianity in practice if not in doctrine had become another magical religion.

Segundo says he believes that in its official teachings the Church successfully avoided turning Christian magic into dogma, but that at the popular level the *ex opere operato* effectiveness of the sacraments, their conferral of grace and their imparting of indelible marks on the soul were almost always understood magically. Thus in practice the relation between the Church and its sacred signs came to be exactly the opposite of what it had originally been: instead of the sacraments building up the Church and pointing to what had to be done in the world, the Church dispensed the sacraments for individuals and pointed to a salvation beyond this world. The result was a sort of "bank-deposit" view of the sacraments, a belief that a sacrament "communicates something that is assumed to be accumulable" in the soul, namely grace.[124]

Nor was this view socially benign, for it allowed for the exploitation of the poor while giving them assurances that they were rich in grace, which was much more important than material possessions. The popular conception of sacraments as magic rites thus allowed them to become instruments of domestication through which the ruling class

---

[122]Segundo, *The Community Called Church*, p. 37.

[123]Segundo, *The Sacraments Today*, p. 21.

[124]Same, p. 92.

(which included the clergy) kept the poor and uneducated masses in many countries economically enslaved and ignorant of the liberative content of the message of Christ. And Segundo contends that this is still true in Latin America today, where "the current sacramental system is a pacifying ideological element which helps to maintain the present status quo of society."[125]

But the situation is not without hope, for in the twentieth century the Church — at least in its official documents — has come to recognize the need to separate itself from the magical attitudes of the past, and Segundo more than once quotes Vatican II to that effect: "A more critical ability to distinguish religion from a magical view of the world and from the superstitions which still circulate purifies religion and exacts day by day a more personal and explicit adherence to faith."[126] In addition, the council's call for social justice in the world, Pope Paul VI's encyclical on *The Development of Peoples*, and the 1968 Medellin Conference at which the bishops of Latin America explicitly called for the full emancipation of the poor from every form of servitude, show that the hierarchy has begun to repudiate the easy identification of the Church with other-worldly salvation.

Segundo applauds this initial institutional turn towards a theology of liberation, but he also cautions that most of the world's Catholic clergy and laity do not yet realize the radical implications of that turn. Thus on the surface there seems to be a crisis in the Church's sacramental life: people are questioning the value of baptism and confession, theologians are reinterpreting the doctrine of the real presence of Christ in the Eucharist, married Catholics are getting divorces, priests are wanting to marry and women are wanting to be priests. But this is only a symptom of a crisis at a deeper level, which "is not a sacramental crisis at all, but a crisis of the ecclesial community itself."[127]

---

[125]Same, p. 112.
[126]*Gaudium et Spes*, no. 7; see Segundo, *The Sacraments Today*, pp. 6, 13.
[127]See Segundo, same, p. 97.

In the end, then, what Segundo offers is not a new, detailed sacramental theology but an entirely new secularist approach to the sacraments based on a radically secular conception of the Church. He does not deny the existence of God or the reality of the incarnation or the need for the sacraments or the power of grace, but he does call for a sweeping reinterpretation of Christian doctrines in this-worldly terms. Seen from such a perspective, the Church is the community of those who are doing God's will, making Christ present in the world and making grace alive in history through their concern for others. The Church's mission is to be a means of salvation for the world by "effectively inserting itself into a love that is already existing, operative and supernatural" so that it "builds up humanity in history."[128] If it does this, then the Church is "the sign of man's fashioning of history in freedom" that God wants it to be;[129] that is, it is a sacrament in a very down-to-earth sense, "a visible community of human beings living in real-life contact with the rest of mankind that, through its existential actions, contains, manifests, and communicates the saving presence of Christ" by contributing toward truly human solutions to economic, political and social problems.

But a Church which is sacramental to the world cannot exist without signs which are sacramental for its members, making God's liberating energy present among them, speaking his prophetic word in their midst, and enabling them to take effective steps towards the establishment of the kingdom.

> On the occasion of each sacrament it should present the Christian people with their present, concrete, existential situation. It should pose this situation as a problem that challenges them and calls for their response. And it should also show divine revelation to be an element capable of helping them to face up to this challenge.

---

[128]Same, p. 7.
[129]Segundo, *Our Idea of God*, p. 79.

The community's response, in turn, must take place on two levels: that of intellectual awareness and understanding, and that of action. When the Christian community organizes itself in sacramental terms, it orients itself toward action designed to meet an historical challenge in a reflective and critical way.[130]

For a liberation approach to the sacraments, maintains Segundo, demands that we "conceive and live and reformuate them in function of a community whose liberative action is secular and historical — as the gospel indicates."[131]

8. Approaches as Models

The existence of four markedly different approaches to the sacraments today (and there are others[132]) naturally leads to the question: Which of these is the correct one? In one sense at least the best answer is: None of them. For all of them are — or are based on — abstract theoretical models, and the sacraments are neither abstract nor theoretical nor models.

Sacraments are not abstractions but concrete realities. They are what Catholics actually do in churches and other places, on Sundays and other days, in the U.S. and other countries. Sacraments are not theories but practices. They involve real people doing real things such as speaking, reading, gesturing, praying, thinking and feeling. Sacra-

---

[130] Segundo, *The Sacraments Today*, p. 104.

[131] Same, p. 93.

[132] Besides the traditional scholastic approach, there have been in history various Protestant and Orthodox accounts of the sacraments; and today there are other Catholic approaches to the sacraments besides these four, for example, liturgical and biblical, pastoral and catechetical, existential and anthropological approaches. For a sample, see the readings at the end of this chapter. The approach of this book is interdisciplinary: Part One draws from psychology, sociology, history and philosophy (i.e., the various philosophical systems behind the current theologies) to shed some light on the sacraments, then Part Two discusses the sacraments with reference to spirituality, pastoral theology, liturgy, ecclesiology and eschatology.

ments are not models but originals. Each instance of sacramental worship is unique and individual, involving different people at different times and places, and displaying a host of other details that can never be exactly repeated.

The initial question in sacramental theology, put very simply, is: What the dickens is going on here? What in the world are all these people doing? And this leads to other questions: Why are they doing these things? What connection do these rituals have with Jesus, with each other, and with similar rituals that Catholics have performed in the past? And finally the fundamental question is: How is God involved here? How are these practices related to the Christian revelation of the divine mystery?

To answer these questions, theologians have to find some intelligent way of pulling the bewildering variety of information about the sacraments (scriptural data, historical records, Christian doctrines, liturgical regulations, findings of psychology and sociology, their own experiences, and so on) into some sort of logically coherent arrangement. When they succeed in doing that, the result is a theory, a theory of the sacraments, a sacramental theology. The theory is abstract because it leaves out or abstracts from the myriad details of sacramental data. And it is a model because in leaving out the details it is something like a sketch which roughly approximates the originals but loses a lot of the originals' richness. So the theoretical model is never the reality; it is always some abstract approximation of it. Moreover, the shape of the model will vary in accordance with the data that it is supposed to cover. Contemporary sacramental theologians, for instance, have more historical data to deal with than the medieval theologians did, and so their models will naturally differ from the older ones in that respect. Similarly, theologians who pay more attention to the texts of the liturgical rites than to the factual experiences of people participating in the sacraments will develop different models than those who do the opposite.

Philosophers today tell us that there are basically two types of models: picture (or representative) models, and disclosure (or interpretative) models.[133] Examples of picture models are things like scale model cars or planes, architects' blueprints and engineers' drawings, geographical globes and maps. Disclosure models are usually less visual and more conceptual. They are things like psychological theories of personality development, scientific explanations of natural phenomena, political models such as democracy and socialism.

To some extent we all use models all the time in our thinking. We all make generalizations from our experience, and then use those generalizations as mental models for interpreting our further experience. For example, we all have a general idea or mental image of a mother or father (role models), a saint or a scoundrel (moral models), a telephone or a typewriter (technological models), and so on, which we have learned and then use to understand the people and things in the world around us. We also get first impressions of the people we meet and the places we visit, and these impressions function as models or frameworks for filling in the details when we learn more about them. We also have a general idea about what our neighborhood looks like, how our business works, and so on, which operates as a model when we need to find our way around in them. Such practical, everyday models can be clear or fuzzy, extremely simple or fairly complex.

Practical everyday models are in some ways both picture models and disclosure models, because they represent realities in our experience for us and they also help us to interpret our further experience. And because we are so familiar with these sorts of models (though of course we do not usually advert to them or realize that they are indeed models), we tend to take theoretical models in the same way. That is, we

---

[133] See Max Black, *Models and Metaphors* (Ithaca, New York: Cornell University Press, 1962) esp. ch. XIII; Frederick Ferré, "Mapping the Logic of Models," in Dallas M. High, ed., *New Essays in Religious Language* (New York: Oxford University Press, 1969) pp. 54-96; Ian T. Ramsey, *Models and Mystery* (London: Oxford University Press, 1964).

tend to take scientific, economic, political and theological theories as pictures of reality. In fact, however, they are not. But because common sense thinking takes them to be pictures of reality, it has a hard time letting go of one model and accepting another. The resistance that people felt about giving up the Ptolemaic theory (the sun goes around the earth) in favor of the Copernican theory (the earth goes around the sun) is a historical case in point. The resistance that many Catholics felt about changes in the liturgy following the Second Vatican Council was the same sort of phenomenon: they had lived with one liturgical model for so long that they took it to be the only true picture of worship.

Since theology is theoretical, however, what it actually contains are not picture models but disclosure models. Most scientists, in both the natural and the human sciences, today regard their theories as disclosure models, and a growing number of Catholic theologians as well accept David Tracy's observation that "theological models do not purport to present exact pictures of the realities they disclose."[134] Rather, they give us general conceptual frameworks within which we can situate and try to understand particular religious realities such as the Church and the sacraments. In Bernard Lonergan's words, models give us "not descriptions of reality, not hypotheses about reality, but simply interlocking sets of terms and relations" which are "useful in guiding investigations, in framing hypotheses and in writing descriptions"[135] of what the Church has done in the past, or of what Catholics are doing today in their sacramental celebrations, for example.

Natural scientists (physicists, chemists, biologists, etc.) can often work within a single large conceptual structure which remains relatively stable even though they have to try out various smaller models for doing new research in partic-

---

[134] David Tracy, *Blessed Rage for Order* (New York: Seabury Press, 1975) p. 22.

[135] Bernard Lonergan, S.J., *Method in Theology* (New York: Herder and Herder, 1972) p. 284, p. 285. For other examples, see Avery Dulles, S.J., *Models of the Church* (New York: Doubleday, 1974), and *Models of Revelation* (New York: Doubleday, 1983).

ular areas. It is only infrequently that natural science experiences massive shifts in its fundamental paradigm or basic structural models.[136] Social scientists on the other hand (psychologists, sociologists, historians, philosophers, etc.) are acutely aware that in their fields the data are so complex and fluid that there is often no single model that they can all agree on and use for interpreting the data on human life. The social or human sciences are for this reason becoming familiar with the practice of using multiple models in their work. And theology is one of the human sciences.

It is true that for the past few centuries Catholic theology relied rather exclusively on one model for its intellectual framework, the model provided by scholastic philosophy, and indeed it seemed so solidly entrenched in our mental landscape that we took it to be a picture model that represented the essential truth about natural and supernatural realities. But as we saw in the introduction to this chapter, before the Middle Ages Catholic thinkers used other models for understanding and interpreting the Christian mysteries. And now in the twentieth century theologians are once again allowing for the possibility of multiple models or alternative theologies to exist side by side. Each model can shed some light on one or another of the Christian mysteries, each can suggest that we look at them from a particular point of view, and each can attempt to describe them in very general terms, but none of them can give us an exhaustive or definitive analysis of those realities. "Theologies do not —or should not — claim to provide pictures of the realities they describe — God, humanity, and world; they can be shown to disclose such realities with varying degrees of adequacy." For theologies give us disclosure or discovery models, and so they "should be taken seriously but not literally."[137]

Such an attitude towards theological models has two important consequences. First, it helps us to overcome the

---

[136]See Thomas Kuhn, *The Structure of Scientific Revolutions* (Chicago: University of Chicago Press, 1962).

[137]Tracy, p. 22.

"model-fixation" which characterized Catholic theology in the past and to some extent still operates in the present. Arguing that the sacraments *are* this and *not* that (e.g., they are causes of grace and not positive prehensions of the Jesus event) is actually a disagreement about theological models and not about the sacraments, and the argument results from accepting one model as usable and rejecting the other as unusable (e.g., accepting the scholastic model and rejecting the process model) for interpreting the sacraments. In fact, this sort of model-fixation (mistaking a single model for the reality) happens both among conservatives who insist on the traditional sacramental theories and reject the newer ones, and among the liberals who declare that some new theory is true and the old ones false. But since the models are abstract and theoretical they are not sacramental realities but ways of interpreting and explaining our individual and social experiences of sacramental worship. They are thus not true or false in themselves but relatively adequate or inadequate for helping us to understanding the sacraments as concrete church practices that we all participate in.

Secondly, this more flexible attitude toward theological models enables us to use different ones at different times, depending on what it is that we want to understand about the sacraments. Disclosure models are interpretative models, giving us a framework within which to situate our personal experience or ecclesiastical practice of sacramental worship, and giving us names for what we find happening within us personally and within us as a community. But disclosure models are also discovery or heuristic models, giving us clues as to what further things there are to be found in sacramental worship — but which we may not yet have experienced or which we as a parish community, for instance, may not yet have put into practice. Sacramental theologies, therefore, are not necessarily models of what *is* going on in some concrete practices; whether or not something happens in or as a result of a particular ritual has to be determined by looking at it through the lens of a particular model, and verifying whether or not what the model focuses on can actually be found in our personal and social experience. Sacramental theologies are therefore better understood as models of what *can be* but *might not be* going on in concrete sacramental practices. And depending on one's doctrinal, liturgical and pastoral orientation, such theologies can provide models of what *should be* or *should not be* going on when Christians gather for sacramental worship.

The existence of multiple models for sacramental theology thus moves us to ask a wider range of questions than we did when we as Catholics accepted and used only one basic model. About any particular sacramental ceremony and about the concrete sacramental practices of a particular group of people we can ask questions such as the following, which are suggested by the experiential, process, charismatic and liberation models: Am I experiencing the presence of Christ? Are we becoming a Christian community? Is my Christian conversion being strengthened and deepened? Is my attitude one of magic or social responsibility? These of course are not the only questions that arise out of these four models, but they indicate the direction that such honest questioning and reflecting on our experience of sacramental worship can go in.

Above all it is important to remember that the models can only help us to ask the questions; they cannot answer the questions. Each model does of course suggest the answers which make the best sense within its own particular framework. But the framework itself cannot give us the answers; it can only help us to locate and interpret the answers. For the answers are not to be found in the models, which are abstract and theoretical, but in the originals, that is, in the concrete experience of the Church's sacramental practices. And this is because it is within the experience of sacramental worship itself that the Christian mystery, or some aspect of it, is disclosed to us.

Recommended Reading

On the four contemporary approaches described in this chapter:

Edward Schillebeeckx, O.P., *Christ, the Sacrament of the Encounter with God* (New York: Sheed and Ward, 1963).

Bernard Lee, S.M., *The Becoming of the Church* (New York: Paulist Press, 1974).

Donald Gelpi, S.J., *Charism and Sacrament* (New York: Paulist Press, 1976).

Juan Luis Segundo, S.J., *The Sacraments Today* (Maryknoll, New York: Orbis Books, 1974).

On other approaches to the sacraments:

Regis Duffy, O.F.M., *Real Presence* (San Francisco: Harper and Row, 1982) develops a foundational approach.

Raymond Vaillancourt, *Toward a Renewal of Sacramental Theology* (Collegeville, Minnesota: Liturgical Press, 1979) is primarily a liturgical approach.

Tad Guzie, *The Book of Sacramental Basics* (New York: Paulist Press, 1981) uses an experiential approach.

William J. Bausch, *A New Look at the Sacraments* (Notre Dame, Indiana: Fides/Claretian, 1977) is a historical and pastoral approach.

Bernard Cooke, *Sacraments and Sacramentality* (Mystic, Connecticut: Twenty-Third Publications, 1983) develops the sociological approach of his earlier articles.

On models:

Ian G. Barbour, *Myths, Models and Paradigms* (New York: Harper and Row, 1974) gives a clear understanding of models and their use in science and religion.

PART TWO: SACRAMENTS TRANSFORMING

In her editor's preface to the volumes in this series, Monika Hellwig has written:

> It seems vitally important for constructive and authentically creative community participation in the shaping of the Church's future life, that a fuller understanding of the sacraments be widely disseminated in the Catholic community.

Knowledge of the psychological, sociological, historical and theological dimensions of religious rituals makes us terribly aware that the sacraments have been and still are shaped by individual and institutional, cultural and even ideological forces. But the opposite is also true, that is, sacraments have a shaping force of their own.

In the past, they have exerted such a force on the individual, communal and institutional life of Catholics and Catholicism. And the same is true today. Sacraments have a transforming effect on those who believe in what they symbolize. They help us to realize more fully who we are, and they call us to actualize what we are not yet. And in doing this, they touch every aspect of our life, from its most intimate dimensions to its most global proportions.

To fully understand the implications of the sacraments, therefore, we need to look at them in a number of contexts, in a series of ever widening theological horizons.

CHAPTER V:
THE SACRAMENTS AND PERSONAL SPIRITUALITY

Every person has a spirit. The question is, whose spirit is it?

This is not a question of uniqueness. Every individual has their own unique spirit — or soul, as the ancients used to call it. Rather, it is a question of type, or sort.

We sometimes ask: What type of person is he? What sort of person is she?

Again, we sometimes say: His spirits are high. Her spirits are low. I'm in good spirits today.

Sometimes we also say: That's a spiritual person. Or even: This is a spiritual place. Here when we say "spirit" we usually mean a religious spirit, a holy spirit, even a Christian spirit.

It is possible, then, to speak of spirit in terms of type, in terms of the sort of spirit that we have, or are.

Christians are supposed to have a spirit which is different from those who have never heard the Gospel. They are supposed to have, and to live in, the spirit of Jesus.

Traditionally in Christianity we have personified the spirit of Jesus, calling it the Holy Spirit. And traditional trinitarian theology has spoken of three "persons" (The original Greek word is *prosopa*, meaning "masks.") in God.

But that trinitarian theology derived, in part, from the fact that many people who saw Jesus in his lifetime perceived in him a spirit which was more than human. It was a divine spirit, God's spirit, or, as we call it today, the Holy Spirit.

And how did they know it was the Holy Spirit? Since they were Jewish and still waiting for the messiah, they weren't yet Christians, and so they hadn't learned it in catechism classes or Sunday school.

They must have learned that Jesus was more than just an ordinary person from the things that he did and said. He touched people's bodies and he touched their hearts, and they were healed physically and spiritually. He spoke to them (and his actions also spoke) and their minds were changed, and so were their lives.

At least some of them were. They were what the gospels call the disciples of Jesus. But the Greek word *mathetes* means something more like "student" in ordinary English. And so we can say that the first followers of Jesus were his students, that is, those who were willing to learn from him.

What they learned from him were not just ideas, concepts. What they learned was the true way to live. St. John writes that Jesus said, "I am the Way, the Truth, and the Life." (Jn. 14:6) An early name for Christianity was "the Way."

Ancient Hebrew had various ways of talking about receiving something spiritual from another person, or from God. Just as the Israelites used the word "breath" (*ruah*) metaphorically to talk about spirit, so also they used another word, another concrete image, to speak about another reality which was just as real but for which they had no abstract word. The reality was that of being spiritually transformed, of being inwardly renewed. To the Israelites it was as though God was "pouring out" his spirit on that person.

Moreover, they imaged the pouring as being done with olive oil, for oil was a precious commodity to a desert people who lived in a dry land, and so they spoke metaphorically of receiving God's spirit as "being anointed," and they spoke of someone who had received that spirit as an "anointed one" (*mashiah*).

The early Jewish followers of Jesus, recognizing that the spirit of God was in him, therefore spoke of him as being anointed and called him "messiah." The equivalent Greek word is *christos* (similar to the word "chrism"), and so the New Testament speaks of *Iesous ho Christos*, Jesus the Anointed One, Jesus the Christ.

The point here, however, is not etymology; it is not the meaning or usage of words. The point is that Jesus showed that he was filled with the spirit of God, and that that is why he was called anointed, or messiah, or Christ.

Even later (though not much), followers of the Way who were living in Antioch were called *Christianoi* or "Christians." (Acts 11:26) In that name-calling there was an implicit recognition that to learn from Jesus meant to share in his spirit, that is, to be anointed with the same spirit with which he had been anointed.

In a number of passages the New Testament speaks of "receiving the spirit" or "receiving the Holy Spirit." (Acts 2:38; 8:14; 19:1-6; 1 Cor. 6:19) It also speaks metaphorically of "being filled with the spirit" or "being anointed by the Holy Spirit" (Acts 2:4; 4:23-31; 6:5-6; 10:44-47; Eph. 1:13) when, for example, the first followers of Jesus laid their hands on others who wanted to become his followers. Many of these passages say, in effect, that the apostles laid their hands on people and they received the Holy Spirit.

A logical question we can ask is: How did the writers of those passages (or before them, the witnesses to those events) know that those people had received the Holy Spirit? There was as yet no theology of baptism or confirmation from which they could draw their ideas.

So the logical answer to that question is: They knew that people had received the spirit of God because these people behaved differently than the way they used to. They exhibited a different spirit in their lives. They lived by the power of some spirit other than the ordinary human one. The way the New Testament writers spoke of it, these people were filled with the spirit of Jesus. They were anointed with the Holy Spirit.

We Catholics today have a sacrament called confirmation. It is a liturgical anointing with oil, and the words of the rite speak of receiving the Holy Spirit. The name itself dates from the early Middle Ages. The Orthodox churches have a parallel sacrament, but it is called chrismation. Both the Eastern ritual and the name (which is closer to the word "Christ") are more ancient. But like the Western ritual, chrismation is understood to be an anointing with the Holy Spirit.

Likewise, all Christians (Catholics, Orthodox and Protestants) have a sacrament called baptism. Now, the Greek word *bapto* in Jesus' time was an ordinary word with an ordinary meaning. It meant "to dip" or "to dunk," or perhaps a little less colloquially, "to immerse." When the early Christians spoke about "being baptized in water," therefore, it may have sounded more to their ears like "being dunked in water." Which is what the ritual was, literally. Today, however, it might sound odd to our ears to speak of the sacrament of dunking, instead of the sacrament of baptism.

But the New Testament also speaks about "baptism in the Holy Spirit." (Mt. 3:11; Acts 1:5; 11:16) Charismatic Christians today also speak about being baptized in the Holy Spirit. In this case, however, it is the word "baptism" which sounds strange to our ears, for we now associate baptism with an ecclesiastical ritual. If we return to the primitive meaning of *baptizo* (a word derived from *bapto*), however, the meaning of the phrase is clear. "Being baptized in the Spirit" means the same as "being immersed in the Spirit." The image is simply the reverse of the anointing image. The one speaks of being covered all over by the Spirit (and the ancient rite of anointing was a liberal smearing with oil over the whole body); the other speaks of being inserted completely into the Spirit (and the ancient rite of baptism was a thorough drenching with water).

Those who used the two metaphors of anointing and immersion were trying to stretch the ordinary meaning of those words (for that is what anyone does, when one resorts to metaphor) to describe something extraordinary. What was extraordinary was something for which there were no ordinary words. It was the extraordinary transformation of a person's spirit which St. Paul referred to in yet another metaphor: putting on Christ. (Gal. 3:27; Eph. 4:24)

Thus baptism and confirmation both point to a profound spiritual reality which today we call by the simple word "conversion." Ancient Greek did have a word for it: *metanoia*. It meant "a change in one's mentality." But conversion is more than a change in thinking. As Donald Gelpi points out, it is also a change in one's feelings or attitudes, and it is also a change in one's way of acting or behaving. Conversion is a thorough change. It involves the whole person. This is what is more fully implied by the metaphors of total immersion and complete anointing.

Besides being a profound (that is, deeply penetrating) reality, therefore, conversion is also a complex reality. It encompasses a transformation of one's entire personality, of one's whole spirit, which shows up as a change in one's thinking, feeling and behaving. For as Rahner reminds us, we symbolize what we are in everything that we do — and thinking and feeling are as much "doings" as physical actions are.

Conversion is also a complex reality because it never ends until we are dead. It may start at some memorable point in time (for example, the moment we said Yes to God, or when we asked Christ to be Lord of our life), but this is not the end of it. We are always finding sections of our personality which we have been unconsciously keeping to ourselves, refusing to allow them to be washed by the Spirit. And if we are growing, we are not always sure whether those new areas of our life will be extensions of our converted or our unconverted self. And sometimes, even those spots which were once anointed mysteriously dry up.

But conversion is also complex because it is of many kinds. One may be converted to a life of crime as well as to a life of charity. One may be converted aesthetically or ethically without being converted religiously. One may be religious without necessarily being Christian (for there are other religions). And one may have experienced a Christian conversion without having become a Catholic Christian (for there are other denominations).

Being a Catholic is therefore more than being ethically converted to doing what is morally good rather than what is pleasant or advantageous. It is more than being religiously converted to God as the ultimate good and the source of life's basic meaning. It is even more than being converted to Christianity, to accepting Christ as the Word of God spoken in human history. It means accepting Christ as he is mediated through a historic tradition of some twenty centuries and a sequence of cultures. It means both coming to know about Christ, and coming to know him, through a church that calls itself Catholic because historically and culturally it *is* catholic.

Historically and through a variety of cultures, Christian conversion has been mediated to people who call themselves Catholics not only through word but also through action, not only through the scriptures but also through the sacraments. This is why the sacraments are said to be part of the Catholic tradition, for *traditio* in Latin means "to hand down" or "to hand over." In other words, conversion to Christ, becoming immersed in him and being anointed in his spirit, has been passed down to us or mediated to us through those special church rituals which we call the sacraments.

But the sacraments are signs; they are symbols of what we are, when we are indeed converted to Christ in a Catholic way; and they are symbols of what we ought to be, when in fact we are not yet converted or not yet as fully converted as we want to be.

The question then becomes: If I call myself a Christian and a Catholic, are these signs symbols of me? Do they symbolize what I have become, and what I am becoming, and what I want to become? Are they authentic symbolizations or externalizations of my present spirit, or are they false symbols of me?

Whether I was baptized as an infant or as an adult, does the fact that I *was* baptized symbolize that I am today immersed in Christ?

Whether I was confirmed as matter of course or as a result of a personal decision, does the fact that I *was* confirmed symbolize that today I live as one anointed with the Holy Spirit?

In a similar way I can ask: If I have been married in the Church or ordained as one of its ministers, does the fact that I *was* thus married or ordained symbolize my present way of being a Christian, either giving myself to another or giving myself in service to others?

Ideally, sacraments effect what they signify. That is, they cause to happen in our lives what it is that they symbolize. But this does not always happen. Even the scholastic theology of the sacraments recognized this, which is why it spoke of the inner disposition which was needed for the fruitful reception of a sacrament. Today's theology also recognizes this, which is why it speaks of conversion and of authenticity in sacramental worship. Scholastic theology also spoke of the reviviscence of a sacrament, which was its own way of talking about what happens in us when, some time after a sacramental action, its meaning hits home, or comes alive for us, and affects our life in a way that it didn't before.

Ideally, however, sacraments should effect what they signify. That is, they should be true symbols of what we already are, and which cause us to become that more fully, since that is what we want to become. The first time that children risk diving off a board, they become, if you will, divers. In some simple, secular way, they have become "converted" from cautious jumpers to more confident individuals. And with every dive that they take after that first one, they both actualize what they have become and become more of what they want to be, what they have decided to become.

So it is with our repeatable sacraments, Eucharist and penance and, when it is appropriate, anointing of the sick. Eucharist (the Greek word from which it comes means "to give thanks") is a true symbol of ourselves only when we come to it in thanksgiving, when we are already grateful for what we have, when we already see it all as gift and not as right, not as something we have earned.

But the Eucharist is also a sacrament composed of many

symbols, not the least of which is sacrifice. It has the power to ritually represent the self-giving that we do every day —but only when that is what we are doing every day. When the words of the liturgy speak of "our sacrifice" they refer to us. It is in the daily giving of ourself to the Father, through meeting the needs of others, that we participate in or become part of Christ's sacrifice. Our worship at Mass can symbolize this, but only if it is already something that we have begun to make real in our life.

We sometimes speak of participation in the liturgy, but authentic participation is not just bodily presence or physical action in the midst of a ritual. It means partaking of its symbolism, letting it represent what we are already a part of, and letting its meaning become part of us, because it signifies what we want to become more fully.

It is the same way with penance or liturgical reconciliation. It is a true symbol for us to the extent that it gathers together the forgiving that we are already doing in our life. If we are already participating in the mystery of reconciliation, of forgiving and allowing ourselves to be forgiven, then taking part in a liturgy of reconciliation can express that authentically and (like the child practicing a new skill) it can give us the inner power we need to become more authentically forgiving persons.

For sacraments are signs of mysteries. (As a matter of fact, the Latin word *sacramentum* was sometimes even used as a translation of the Greek word *mysterion*.) But the mysteries are not "out there," removed from us. When we encounter them, when we consciously confront them, they are undeniably larger than we are. But they are also so close that we are experientially touching them, or being touched by them. Whether the mystery is that of Christ's presence, or the Father's graciousness, or the Spirit's healing of hearts and relationships, or whatever, — whenever it is truly encountered it is experienced as already there, an encompassing reality into which we are somehow inserted. In this sense only is it "out there." But if it is not also "in here," if it is not already becoming part of us and if we are not already becoming part of it, then a sacrament signifies nothing that is real as far as we ourselves are concerned.

The repetition of some sacraments ought to have a cumulative effect in our life. Like the children who practice their skills through repetition, repeating the symbols of what we are to some extent but not fully enables us to live into the mystery that they symbolize. Like children who are so exuberant about what they have learned that they do it over and over gain, repeating a symbol of what we have become can also be a celebration of the mystery that is becoming a real part of our life. But like children who are sometimes content with what they have learned and are not interested in developing their skills, repeating the symbols can become lifeless, a dull redoing of a duty. For sometimes like children who give in to pressure from their peers, we repeat our sacraments not because they truly express us or because they truly present us with what we desire, but because the Church tells us to do them.

Dull repetition, however, is not the attitude of a learner, a student, a disciple. In and through our sacraments (though of course these are not the only ways) we ought to be expressing the conversion of our inner spirit to that of Christ's spirit. They should be a means through which that conversion is continued in our life, through which our discipleship is made more complete. They should be moments of liminality in which we allow ourselves to let go of the spirits of self-seeking and self-sufficiency, of bitterness and competition, of division and alienation, and in which we enter into dialogue with the Lord who reveals to us a different spirit, a spirit of trusting dependence on God, of befriending cooperation with others, of integrating unity with both.

To be truly effective in our lives, our sacraments should symbolize what we are already living: our daily dying to whatever it is that robs us and others of the fulness of life, and our daily rising to a newer, more abundant life; our awareness of the miraculous wonder that is life itself; our acknowledgment of everything, absolutely everything, as gift, for there is nothing that we have entirely earned (though we may have worked hard for some of it); our participation in the mysteries of transcendent reconciliation, of psychical and physical healing, of the transformation of our inner and outer life, of our experienced unity with God and our empowerment by a divine spirit which is not ours but which is becoming ours as we become immersed in it.

If this happens, and to the extent that it happens, we become truly disciples of Jesus, for we are learning his way of living and being, we are becoming anointed with the same spirit that anointed him and made him Christ for us. And to that extent we also become Christ for others, signs of what God can do in a person's life, and therefore sacraments of human salvation in the world.

Recommended Reading

Regis A. Duffy, O.F.M., *Real Presence: Worship, Sacraments and Commitment* (San Francisco: Harper and Row, 1982).

Joseph M. Powers, S.J., *Spirit and Sacrament* (New York: Seabury Press, 1973).

Francois-Xavier Durrwell, C.SS.R., *The Eucharist: Presence of Christ* (Denville, New Jersey: Dimension Books, 1974).

Bernard Haring, C.SS.R., *The Sacraments and Your Everyday Life* (Liguori, Missouri: Liguori Publications, 1976).

Bernard Bro, O.P., *The Spirituality of the Sacraments* (New York: Sheed and Ward, 1968).

CHAPTER VI:
THE SACRAMENTS AND COMMUNAL SPIRITUALITY

Some parishes are dead, lifeless; others have spirit. The difference is tangible.

You can feel the difference when you talk to the parishioners. You can sense it even by reading the Sunday bulletin. You can tell it at Mass, by the way people say the responses or sing the hymns, and by the way they hang around and talk to each other — or rush off silently to their cars — afterwards.

But spirit in a community is not just on or off, present or absent. There are different types of spirits. Get to know a parish better and you begin to recognize a pervading spirit in the place. Sometimes it is haughty and proud; sometimes it is weak and timid; sometimes it is a spirit of wealth and self-sufficiency; sometimes it is a spirit of destitution and desperation; sometimes it shows itself as a concern for children and their education; sometimes it shows itself as an awareness of global politics and economic issues.

In a large parish with many weekend liturgies, the spirit of the Saturday evening crowd is different from that of the early Sunday morning few, and both are different from the spirit of the groups that regularly attend the other Masses. Sometimes there are specialized communities within the parish: the Catholic school parents and kids, the CCD parents and kids; the elderly and the old faithfuls, the young marrieds and the new arrivals; the teenagers, the college students, the working singles; the cursillistas and the charismatics; the Knights of Columbus, and the Altar and Rosary Society; and don't forget the bingo crowd.

Still, having discerned these different spirits, the question we must always ask is: Whose spirit is it? Is it the spirit of Jesus? Is it a welcoming, affirming, strengthening, forgiving, healing, unifying spirit? Is it a sanctifying spirit, a holy spirit? Or is it some other spirit?

We catch a glimpse of the spirit of the early Christian community in the idyllic picture painted by St. Luke:

> The whole group of believers was united, heart and soul; no one claimed for his own use anything that he had, as everything they owned was held in common.... None of their members was ever in want, as all those who owned land or houses would sell them, and bring the money from them, to present it to the apostles; it was then distributed to any members who might be in need. (Acts 4:32, 34f)
>
> These remained faithful to the teaching of the apostles, to the brotherhood, to the breaking of the bread and to prayer. The many miracles and signs worked through the apostles made a deep impression on everyone.... They went as a body to the Temple every day but met in their houses for the breaking of bread; they shared their food gladly and generously; they praised God and were looked up to by everyone. Day by day the Lord added to their community those destined to be saved. (Acts 2:42f, 46f)

Indeed it was an idyllic picture. Modern exegetes piece together a more realistic picture from other direct and indirect evidence found in the New Testament, such as the scolding that St. Paul gives the Corinthians in his first letter to them, or such as the warnings that Jesus addresses to his disciples in the gospels.

Nevertheless, ideals have a reality of their own, and it is not to be treated lightly. Ideals (of whatever sort they might be) set standards which we try to live up to, and they give us norms against which we measure ourselves. They give us images which govern our thinking, feeling, and acting. When presented in story form — such as the Bible or any book within it, or such as the life of Christ or any of Jesus' parables — they give us pictures within which we can situate and interpret our own life story.

None of us, however, live entirely within the Jesus story; all of us fail to completely live up to our Christian ideals. Sometimes the failure is deliberate, more often it is unintentional. But it is nonetheless real, so we notice the difference between our real ideals and our real lives. We call that gap, that falling short, sin. The Greek word for sin in the New Testament, means, literally, "missing the mark."

When we fail to live up to our ideals, we tend to do one of two things. Either we change our lives, or we change our ideals. When our ideals are private standards that we have set for ourselves, it is easy to lower or even switch our standards. But when our ideals are those that we hold in common with others, doing that is not so easy. Often the only realistic way to remove ourselves from the group's norms is to remove ourselves from the group. When the group is large enough, however, another alternative is to escape into anonymity: to hide our shortcomings, and hope that no one will notice.

For the community that calls itself Christian, the norms are set by the New Testament, and in particular by the words and example of Christ. Since the early days of the apostolic community, these norms have been kept alive through preaching and teaching, exhortation and example; and it was this community, despite its human shortcomings, that preserved the story and the message of Jesus for decades before they were written down and canonized as scriptural. Ever since then, scriptural norms have been primary in the Christian Church.

For the community that also calls itself Catholic, morever, Christian ideas and ideals have also been kept alive from the beginning in the Church's sacramental worship. *Lex orandi, lex credendi* is an ancient maxim: what we pray is what we believe. As a matter of fact, much of what is found in the gospels was preserved within the early community by being told and retold at times of common prayer. And some of the Church's official sacraments had informal roots in Christian practice before they were given ecclesiastical form. Marriage and the anointing of the sick are the two clearest examples of this, but a case could also be made for ordination and reconciliation.

What we as Christians find in the Bible, therefore, is first of all a kerygmatic and prophetic revelation of who we are and what we are called to be. It is kerygmatic (from the Greek *kerygma*, meaning "proclamation") because it is a public announcement, made for all to hear. The facts and the ideals that it discloses are not private standards that individuals may take or leave, but realities and values that have a transcendent truth and validity. It is prophetic (from the Greek *propheteuo*, meaning "to speak on behalf of") because it is God's word spoken in the midst of the community. It reveals what God wants us to hear, not about there and then, but about here and now.

Similarly, what we as Catholics find in the sacraments is the same kerygmatic and prophetic revelation. This is obviously true of our Eucharistic worship, which is founded on the gospel command of Christ to do this in his memory, and in which we hear God's scriptural word prophetically proclaimed in our midst. Most of the other sacramental rites also contain scripture readings, but we should not overlook the fact that the sacramental actions themselves have a message for us. Those actions in some way speak louder than words, especially when we are not passive observers but active participants in the rituals, for they immediately affect our behavior; and through repetition over weeks and years and generations, they influence our perduring attitudes and inclinations. The sacraments thus prophetically proclaim God's living word, for in them the divine reality and its norms are lived out in human gestures, and through them we come to perceive the mystery of which they are a revelation.

Now of course there is a sense in which all this is a bunch of baloney. A lot of times we read the Bible or hear it read in church, and we get nothing out of it. Just as often we go to Mass or attend a wedding or a baptism and the same thing happens — at least as far as any prophetic proclamations are concerned. We are like the people in the gospels who look but do not see, who hear but do not understand. So perhaps it would be truer to say, from the viewpoint of our experience at least, that the scriptures and the sacraments ought to be kerygmatic prophecies for us, instead of suggesting that this is what they always are for us.

When the sacraments do speak to us, however, we find ourselves addressed simultaneously in two different manners: we are addressed as individuals, and as members of a group. As individuals we hear ourselves called to discipleship in one or more of the many ways that were discussed in the last chapter. And as members of a group we hear ourselves called to community in one or more parallel ways.

First and foremost, then, our sacramental actions call us (if we are sensitive to what they are symbolically saying to us) simply to be a community. The very fact that we are gathered together around common symbols in which we all profess belief unites us in some rudimentary yet fundamental ways. The fact that we repeat words and gestures in unison (often speaking in the first person plural: "We give thanks...", "Our Father...", etc.) both consciously and subconsciously suggests that we should be living up to what we are calling ourselves, namely, a "we" group, a community. And the fact that we repeat these symbolic rituals together periodically tells us without saying it outright that we should accept the others in the group into the rhythm of our lives, and that not to do so is somehow dishonest.

Secondly, our sacramental actions call us to enter into the mysteries that they symbolize. When we attend baptisms we hear ourselves called to be an accepting and believing community. At confirmations we find ourselves asked to be a supportive and strengthening community. At penance services we recall that we should be a forgiving and reconciling community. At weddings we are reminded that we should be faithful and loving in a particular way to our spouse and family. At ordinations we are reminded of our collective call to discipleship and service within and beyond the Church. When we participate in an anointing of the sick we hear ourselves being asked to be a healing and hopeful community. And when we attend the Eucharistic liturgy, through its rich and complex symbolism we are called to be a community in many ways, but especially in a way that unites itself with the dying and rising of Christ.

Moreover, the prophetic call of the sacraments comes to us both overtly and covertly. Overtly we are sometimes asked in the sacramental rites to publicly assent to what the sacraments symbolize, and we often pray for the grace to be what we are supposed to be as Christians. But more subtly, the rituals proceed on the assumption that those who are attending them are already what they are supposed to be; that is, the rites are written in a way that presumes that those who join in them are already a faithful, loving, hopeful, serving, healing and reconciling people. And so we find ourselves facing an existential gap between what we are presumed to be if we call ourselves a Church and what we know we actually are. But if we allow ourselves to be pulled into that gap, we suddenly find ourselves attracted to and stretching toward the other side, the side of what we are not yet but ought to be. And it is in that liminal moment that we hear most clearly God's prophetic call to self-transcendence.

Unfortunately, however, community like conversion is not simple but complex. There are, of course, the complexities of every concrete situation: the people involved and their individual personalities, their particular gifts and hopes, shortcomings and fears, their moral and intellectual and emotional maturity or lack of it. But in addition to these there is the complexity of community itself. For community can exist on many different levels, and so the call to be a Christian community is an invitation to a multileveled unity embracing common experiences, common ideas, and common values.

People can be united in common experience. Even total

strangers thrown together by a natural disaster can find themselves open toward and cooperative with each other. The bond that holds a family together, or gives a small town its identity, or provides the motivation for class reunions, is largely an experiential bond. By sharing — or having shared — a common experience, people are united in a community of feelings and images through which they perceive themselves as having something basic in common.

People can also be united in common ideas. Again, even total strangers can find themselves open and at ease with one another once they discover that they share common beliefs and assumptions. They find that they can communicate at the idea level even if their personal backgrounds are different, and even if their plans for utilizing those ideas are different. A lot of shop talk is based on this sort of intellectual commonality, as are classroom discussions and professional meetings or conventions. A common basis in understanding makes it possible for people to understand others and to make themselves understood by others.

Finally, people can be united in common decisions and in the actions which flow from those decisions. Even total strangers at a political demonstration, for example, can find themselves united in a common purpose. When they start a conversation with each other they may find that their backgrounds and motivations for coming are quite different, though they still agree on a common goal or course of action. A common decision — even the open-ended decision that something has to be done — can join people in a community of action and social interaction.

Now all too often, it seems, Catholics are strong on community at the middle level and weak on community at the other two levels. We tend to feel (or at least we act as if it were true) that we have a community if we all believe the same things. We call people Catholics when they believe what Catholics are supposed to believe, and we call them other names (Protestants, Buddhists, atheists, and so on) if they believe something else. Very often the preaching that we hear at Mass and the teaching that we hear in school are focused on what we should or should not believe. And even in our sacramental worship the emphasis is often on what we believe about God, about ourselves, and about what is happening in and through the ritual.

But this emphasis on belief just as often robs our sacramental symbols of their truth and effectiveness. At the very least it denies much of the existential truth and depletes much of their potential effectiveness. For how can our symbols speak the truth about our lives unless we are actually living it? And how can they truly express what we intend to do unless we actually do it?

If we ask these sorts of questions with reference to our personal spirituality we easily see their validity. For example, if I go to communion and I neither experience the presence of Christ nor intend to unite myself with his redemptive suffering, isn't my ritual gesture somewhat empty and ineffective? Or if I go to confession neither having asked forgiveness nor intending to be reconciled with others, isn't my symbolic action somewhat meaningless and futile?

In the same way, then, we can ask those same kinds of questions about ourselves as a community. For sacraments, as symbolic rituals, are not just kerygmatic and prophetic statements of what we are called to be. First and foremost they are meant to be symbolic expressions of what we truly are. This is why, when we are not living up to the ideal that they hold forth for us, they have a certain prophetic power. We implicity recognize that they ought to be symbolic of what we are, even when we are not yet what they symbolize.

But what we are is not just our ideas. It is not just what we are thinking. As Bernard Lee observes from his process perspective, an awful lot of what we are comes from our environment through our experience; we prehend it into ourselves, as it were, and so our past becomes an element in our present selves. We form a society that becomes together, therefore, only when we have common experiences — especially experiences of each other — as the foundation of our common growth. We form an experiential community, in other words, to the extent that we are united on the level of experience.

Likewise, what we are is not just our thoughts but our actions. As Karl Rahner suggests, from a phenomenological viewpoint our actions are living symbols of our inner selves. Our decisions spring from our innermost beliefs and convictions (whether or not these correspond to the things that we *say* we believe in), and our actions flow from our decisions. And so we become a community that is joined together on the level of values only to the extent that we share common decisions and common courses of action. They may be essentially the same decisions that we could and would make singly, but unless we make and carry them out together they do not join us to each other in community.

Now it is clear, both from the words of our liturgical rites, and from the nature of religious ritual itself, that our sacraments call us to be a multileveled community, even as they call us individually to complete conversion and not just a change in ideas. It is only when we interact with each other on all three of these levels that we truly become a community at worship (as opposed to an audience of spectators) and that we can honestly call ourselves a community (as opposed to giving ourselves a euphemistic label).

This means that in order to be a community at worship we must first of all be a community. And in order to be a community at Christian worship we must first of all be a Christian community. In other words, the things that we have in common must be things that are specifically Christian. And at least some of the things that make us specifically Christian are precisely those things that the Catholic sacraments are intended to signify.

The sacraments in traditional theology were considered to be signs of the Christian mysteries. Because of the emphasis on the intellectual component of our faith, the mysteries were often taken to be beliefs such as the incarnation, the trinity and so on. But these in fact are not the mysteries that the sacraments signify and are supposed to celebrate. Rather, what the sacraments directly signify are those mysteries as they are found in the life of the Church. This is why Rahner and others can speak of sacraments as expressions of the Church's nature. But it is only when that nature is alive in a given group of human beings that the sacraments can outwardly express what those persons inwardly are as a Christian community, as a Church.

Another traditional way of speaking about the sacraments was to say that they derive their effectiveness from participating in the realities that they signify. Again here we have sometimes taken this to mean that the Mass derives its efficacy from Christ's sacrifice, or that penance puts us in contact with God's forgiveness, and so on. All well and good, but today we can also ask: How does this actually happen? What is the concrete meaning of those abstract formulas?

Concretely, what those theological statements mean is that the realities which the sacraments signify must be existentially present in the worshipping community, and if they are in fact present then the sacraments are effective in more than just a kerygmatic and prophetic sense. Pope Paul VI in his encyclical on the Eucharist called it the *mysterium fidei*, the mystery of faith. The same could be said of all the other sacraments as well, for in every truly sacramental celebration two elements must be present: the mystery and faith. It is not the faith, however, that makes the mystery present; that would be mere psychologism or autosuggestion. Rather it is in faith that we recognize the presence of the mystery, acknowledge its reality, and name it in some fashion. And this implies that the mystery must already be present.

Again, traditional theology spoke of the sacraments as causing their effects *ex opere operato*, through the performance of the sacred ritual itself. Our tendency as Catholics has been to interpret this medieval formula in rather mechanical terms which suggest that the sacraments work automatically, without any human contribution. But this interpretation does not adequately express the insight of the medieval theologians who first gave us that phrase. What they perceived was that when sacraments are effective, their effectiveness does not depend on who the minister is (or how holy he is) but on what the Church does. For at bottom the sacraments are not the work of a minister (*opus operantis*) but the work of the Church, of the Christian community.

If we recast that medieval insight in more modern terms, the *ex opere operato* concept is quite plausible. By ordaining a man a priest, for instance, a Christian community empowers him to be a sacramental minister for them. He thus receives through this ritual a "priestly character" which thereafter distinguishes him from nonordained Christians. Likewise, when children are baptized they enter a community which communicates its own spirit to them, a spirit of faith, hope and love which empowers them to be saved from sin, that is, to become like Christ. They thus receive through that ritual a "baptismal character" which thereafter distinguishes them from unbaptized persons, or persons who are not immersed in the community. Similarly, when people go to confession they receive the forgiveness of God from the Church, that is, from the community. And having been thus forgiven, they receive the spiritual power that they need to live free from that sin in the future.

This same sort of existential analysis could be given for each of the other sacraments. But in all these cases we would continue to see that the sacramental reality (*sacramentum et res*), as it was called, although it comes ultimately from God, comes proximately from the community, and it is this mysterious reality which is signified and made concretely present through the sacramental ritual, that is, *ex opere operato*.

When we look at the sacraments concretely and existentially, therefore, we must say that it is not the sign that makes the sacramental reality present, but rather it is the presence of the reality that makes the sign sacramental. It is when those mysterious realities are present in the community — realities which in human terms we can designate as acceptance, forgiveness, love, healing, trust, empowerment, support, hope, and so on — that they can be truthfully and effectively symbolized in sacramental ritual. And it is when those realities are present in an uncommonly noticeable degree that we as Christians find ourselves compelled to admit that they are not our doing but God's, that they are not "natural" but "supernatural" mysteries. Yet actually, their presence to any degree is a gift of God, and in that sense a grace, which may be recognized and named as such by those who have faith.

Moreover, the specifically Christian mysteries are those which are revealed to us through the life, death and resurrection of Jesus: having a living relationship to God as Father, perceiving his Word spoken in our midst, being empowered by his Spirit in our hearts, surrendering everything we thought was important and thus discovering what is truly valuable, living under the liberating reign of God rather than under the enslaving rule of sin, and so on. These are the very same mysteries which are disclosed to us through the sacraments, and whose very disclosure reinforces them in our lives. This becomes more evident once we remember that the sacraments, like the scriptures, often speak of these mysteries not in such general but in theologically specific terms: love of enemies (reconciliation), the call to discipleship (ordination), receiving the Spirit (confirmation), and so on.

The basic question that we must ask ourselves as a community celebrating the Christian mysteries is, therefore: Are those mysteries present among us simply as common beliefs, or also as common experiences, and also as communally lived out values? With reference to the seven ecclesiastical sacraments our questioning can become more specific.

Baptism is a sacrament of initiation, bringing incorporation into the Church and separation from the sinfulness that contaminates the world, and bestowing the basic gifts of faith, hope and love. As a parish community we can ask ourselves: To what extent are we a recognizable community into which the ritual action marks a real initiation? Do we truly incorporate that infant or adult into our common life? Will those who are baptized be any more free from sin than if they had not been baptized? How do they receive faith, hope and love from the other members of the community?

Confirmation is a celebration of a fuller reception of the same Spirit which was once received through baptism. But as a parish do we really give those who are confirmed any more of our spirit than we did before? What do we do to strengthen their faith, to raise their hopes, to deepen their ability to love? Are we spiritually empowering them to be more mature Christians, to participate more fully in the death and resurrection of Christ? How are we enabling them to become disciples of Jesus, learners of his way of living, witnesses to each other, servants within and beyond the community?

Eucharist is a sacramental celebration of our unity with Christ and with each other, of our openness to and reception of God's word, of our identification with the death and resurrection of Jesus. As a parish we can ask: Is there really a unity here to be celebrated? To what extent are we openly receiving God's word on other days besides Sunday, by reading the scriptures and studying them together, by sharing with each other what God speaks to us in our own hearts, by seeing his word uttered in the example of the community? How do we willingly die with confident hope of resurrection, individually and communally sacrificing our time and money, our self-interest and ambition, so that others may live, and in doing so discover that we ourselves are born to new life?

Penance is a ritual symbolization of God's forgiveness and our reconciliation with one another. Is that forgiveness also present and alive in our parish? Are we a reconciled and reconciling community, taking the initiative to forgive others and asking their forgiveness? What are we doing to make it possible for adults and even children (not to mention parents and teenagers) to become reconciled with one another, to learn to live in the spirit of forgiveness?

Anointing is a sacramental sign of spiritual and physical healing. Do we as a parish community bring that healing to one another at other times as well? Are we alert and responsive to the hurt of neglected and abused children, to the anxieties of adolescents, to the problems and frustrations of families, to the loneliness of the bedridden and the aged?

Are we meeting the needs of those who are sick or poor or handicapped or out of work?

Marriage is a ceremony that symbolizes the intimate relation between Christ and the Church, and that initiates two persons into that same sort of self-giving relationship. Can we honestly ask engaged couples to take as the model for their future life together the present relationship between our parish and our Lord? Are we a living witness to what a married life of fidelity, intimacy and service ought to be? What are we as a larger community doing to prepare young people and empower families to be smaller but no less real Christian communities?

Ordination is a sacramental calling and initiation to ministry in the Church. Are we as a parish a ministering community? Are we individually and collectively engaged in ministering to the spiritual and physical, personal and social, religious and Christian needs of our parish and the people in it? Do we encourage and praise service within the community so that some, at least, are enabled to choose ministry as their life's work?

These are but some of the specific questions that we as members of Christian communities must ask ourselves if our sacraments are to be truly symbolic and truly effective. If our sacraments are truly symbolic they have to participate in the realities that they symbolize, that is, they have to be a living extension, an outgrowth of Christian mysteries which are already being experienced and believed and acted out in our midst. And if they are indeed truly symbolic in this way, then they will be truly effective; for as symbolic actions they will intensify our appreciation and understanding of the mysteries that they represent, as repeated actions they will constantly recall us to an awareness and response to those mysteries, and as communal actions they will unite us in a common involvement with and commitment to their life-giving effects on us.

If our sacramental celebrations are genuinely symbolic, in other words, they will be truly sacramental and truly celebrations. They will be truly sacramental for they will not only express the mysteries that they signify but they will also draw us into them, transforming us in the process. They will be not only expressing community at all three levels but also creating community at all those levels. They will be, to use St. Paul's phrase, building up the body of the Lord in strength and unity.

When this happens, there will be less danger that the sacraments will be seen as some sort of magic, except in that wonderfully childlike sense in which everything is marvelous and sparkles with mystery. There will also be little danger that the sacraments will be thought of as automatically effective, except in that authentically existential sense in which inner vitality is spontaneously life-giving. And there will be less temptation to be careless in our sacramental celebrations, except in that healthy and mature sense in which concern for what is central frees us from worrying about what is peripheral.

For when our sacraments are truly expressive of our spirit, and when our spirit is the Holy Spirit of our Lord, they are at one and the same time effects and causes of our being a Christian community.

Recommended Reading

William Bausch, *A New Look at the Sacraments* (Notre Dame, Indiana: Fides/Claretian, 1977).

Tad Guzie, *The Book of Sacramental Basics* (New York: Paulist Press, 1981).

Leonard Foley, O.F.M., *Signs of Love* (Cincinnati: St. Anthony Messenger Press, 1976).

Donald L. Gelpi, S.J., *Charism and Sacrament* (New York: Paulist Press, 1976).

G. M. A. Jansen, O.P., *The Sacramental We* (Milwaukee: Bruce Publishing Company, 1968).

CHAPTER VII:
THE SACRAMENTS AND ECCLESIAL SPIRITUALITY

In his modern classic, *The Spirit of Catholicism*, Karl Adam endeavored to define what made the Roman Church catholic and to explain how it was different from other Christian churches. Both in the title and in the book he called attention to the fact that being a Catholic means possessing and being possessed by a distinctive religious spirit.

If you talk about religion with other Christians, you soon discover that there is a certain flavor or style to being a Catholic that is different from that of being a Protestant, no matter what the denomination. If you read confessional theologians or listen to the sermons of Protestant ministers, you often sense an attitude and mentality that underlies an other than Catholic way of being Christian. And if you attend Protestant services or Orthodox liturgies, you discover that there is a spirit about them which is somehow dissimilar from the spirit of Catholicism.

In ecumenical circles, the Catholic Church is sometimes referred to as a "liturgical" church. In this way it is similar to the high Anglican and Eastern Orthodox churches, which also put a great deal of emphasis on traditional rituals of public worship. The "non-liturgical" churches for the most part build their church services around the scriptures, give less attention to rituals such as the sacraments, and are generally less concerned with ecclesiastical traditions. One aspect of the spirit of Catholicism, then, is its continuing insistence that traditional church rituals (in particular the sacraments) express, maintain and foster what it is as a Christian institution.

Speaking very broadly, any church — indeed any religion — is sacramental. Karl Rahner uses the phenomenological analysis of symbolism to show that the Church is necessarily sacramental inasmuch as it expresses itself in symbolic forms, that is, it externalizes its inner nature in words and actions which make that nature something real and concrete in the world and at the same time make it visible or tangible to people. This is true of any church or any religion, for it is clear that this general phenomenological description fits any social institution whatsoever: by doing what it does, it expresses what it is. And because social as well as individual actions are unavoidably symbolic, it is possible to perceive the inner spirit of a church through the public actions which manifest that spirit.

One can plausibly argue, as Catholic theologians do, that the sacraments are the expressions of the Church *par excellence*. Sociologists might object that this perspective is too narrow since it leaves many social, economic, political, historical and organizational factors out of consideration. Protestant theologians also might object that such an approach does not give sufficient attention to preaching the word, to individual and social witness to Christ, or to other non-liturgical dimensions of their churches. But Catholicism as a liturgical church has traditionally maintained and continues to assert that it is first and foremost a community of believers who encounter God in and through that system of rituals known as the sacraments. Granting then that other things could be said about the nature of the Church from other perspectives, it is certainly legitimate for Catholics to examine their sacraments for some insight into the essence of Christianity as it is found in their own ecclesiastical tradition.

What then is the spirit of Catholicism as it is embodied and symbolized in its liturgical rituals?

Beginning from the wider perspective of the Church's entire sacramental system, or the Church's liturgical life in general, we can say that the spirit of Catholicism is an incarnational one, which in turn implies that it stretches vertically in a transcendental direction and horizontally in a historical direction.

We are an incarnational church. We accept the Pauline description of ourselves as the body of Christ, the continuing incarnation of Christ in the world. In the Church as an institution, in our various ecclesiastical institutions, and specifically in our liturgical institutions, the spirit of Christ is embodied and made visible. St. Augustine in the fourth century defined sacraments as signs of sacred realities, but Catholic theologians in our own century have called our attention to the fact that the Church itself is fundamentally a sacrament, for it is a visible sign of the reality of God. As such it is a sacrament that underlies all the other sacraments, which are liturgical manifestations of the Church's basically sacramental nature. Through its rituals it reveals what it is, what the message of Jesus is, and what Christians are called to be.

Being an incarnational church, we are in our sacraments a worshipping church. We accept the Second Vatican Council's description of ourselves as the people of God, a community of persons who are receptive and responsive to the self-revelation of the transcendent Person. St. Thomas Aquinas in the thirteenth century argued that sacraments are necessary because human beings need signs for communication: we communicate to others and receive their communications to us only through the medium of signs. If therefore we are to receive God's communication to us it must come through signs. Almost spontaneously we think of this in terms of visible signs, words, and especially the words of scripture. But St. Thomas' argument causes us to pause and reflect on the fact that through those peculiar signs called sacraments, what God is communicating to us is not ideas but divine life. Apart from the Eucharistic liturgy they do not contain very much in the way of verbal communication, and the basic traditional teaching about the sacraments is that they are instruments of God's grace. In our sacramental rituals we become receptive to that almost ineffable energy which we sometimes name sanctifying grace or even the Holy Spirit itself. Having opened ourselves up to that transcendent vitality, we respond by allowing it to permeate our attitudes and affectivity, by letting it convert our intentions and govern our actions, and in so doing we become what we call ourselves: God's people. Not that we deny that those who are not in the Church can also receive and respond to God's self-revelation in other ways; but as a church we stand for the fact that sacramental worship is a primary focus of transcendental communication.

Moreover, as an incarnational church we are also a historical church. We accept the Israelite insight that time is not cyclical but directional, and we embrace as our own the whole of history from the creation to the parousia. More specifically we trace the history of ours and the world's salvation from before the time of Jesus, through the apostolic and patristic periods, through the Dark Ages and the medieval period, through the Renaissance and modern times, through the present and into the future. Our church history alone spans almost twenty centuries, and it is a history not only of theological speculation and ecclesiastical politics but also of liturgical worship. We see ourselves as the church founded by Christ, in the line of the apostles, bringing Christian baptism to the ends of the earth, celebrating the Eucharist in diverse ways down through history, reconciling the repentant, comforting the sick and the dying, sanctifying family life and ministering to the Christian community not just as individuals but as an institution, as a church. The history of Catholicism as an incarnational church, in other words, is from a sacramental perspective the historical mediation of divine life into human lives. It has been an imperfect mediation, to be sure, blemished as it has sometimes been with dogmatism and fanaticism, provincialism and superstition. We can be chagrined and even ashamed at what has sometimes passed for Christian worship. But the Catholic spirit is not to deny the past but to acknowledge it, the bad with the good, to attempt to discern the one from the other, and to affirm that sacramental worship is and will continue to be a primary means of transcendental communication.

Narrowing our perspective now, we can briefly examine the seven ecclesiastical rituals historically designated as sacraments to see what they reveal about the spirit of Catholic Christianity.

The one sacrament which touches on all the others both historically and theologically is holy orders. The sacrament is so named because it covers various orders or levels of ministry in the Church, and historically the administration or celebration of all the other sacraments has been connected with those in ministerial orders. Theologically the sacrament of orders is related to the others through the notion of mediation, the idea that the divine life is communicated into human lives through the sacramentality of human actions. Traditionally we have trained and ordained specific individuals to minister to Christians through sacramental rituals, but the theological implications of this practice are much broader than the fact that we are a church with ministers called priests; it implies that we are a priestly church. As an institution we stand committed to the principle that ministry is a mediation of transcendent reality, to the concept of service as a Christian vocation, and to the practice of empowering individuals to perform the service of sacramental mediation in the Church.

A sacrament which touches the lives of all Catholics in one way or another is marriage. Academically one can debate whether the sacrament is the wedding ritual or the union of two persons in wedded life, but ecclesiologically this makes little difference since the meaning of Christian marriage in both instances is the same. Having endowed marriage with a church ceremony since the twelfth century, we have institutionally ratified what St. Paul said in the first century, namely that the ideal marital relationship is one of unending fidelity and self-sacrificing love. Such a relationship is truly Christian for it symbolizes the relationship between Christ and the Church: self-donation and loving obedience to the Father's will. As an institution which symbolizes what it stands for in its rituals, therefore, we take that relationship as a paradigm of communal love, primarily for the natural family but by extension in the spiritual family which is the Church.

A sacramental means of maintaining and regaining that sort of relationship whenever it is lost is the sacrament of reconciliation, officially known as penance. The name derives from the Latin word *paenitentia* which is often translated as "penitence" but which is closer in meaning to the Greek word *metanoia* in its sense of "conversion." Quite obviously conversion — or more accurately here, reconversion — to loving God and caring for others can take place outside a liturgical context. But by retaining a sacrament of reconciliation within our liturgical tradition we say in deed as well as in words that we are, and are committed to being, a forgiving community, a reconciling church.

Sacramentally too we express our belief that we are and are committed to being a healing community in the anointing of the sick. Very early in our history this anointing was done by ordinary Christians for themselves and others; later as a liturgical ritual its administration was reserved to the clergy; still later its reception was restricted to those who were so sick that they were at the point of dying, and so its name for a few centuries was extreme unction, the last anointing. Throughout all these variations, however, anointing as a sacramental ritual has expressed our ecclesial faith in the power of God to touch and transform people's lives, not just spiritually but even physically. And it has said that we are to be channels of God's healing power not just singly as individuals but also collectively as a church.

Another sacrament of strengthening, though in a somewhat different sense, is confirmation. This particular ritual of anointing dates back to the ancient rite of Christian initiation. Although the name of the sacrament comes to us from the early Middle Ages (when it was separated from baptism and hence needed a separate name), in the patristic period it signified through the action of the bishop a spiritual empowerment that came with full membership in a ministering, loving, forgiving and healing community. Even later, when the sacrament was given a more individualistic interpretation, it still represented a strengthening of the spirit that is available through active adult membership in the Church.

As the basic sacrament of Christian initiation, baptism has an inescapably ecclesial meaning. As with confirmation its meaning was for a long time privatized so that it was looked at as a means of individual salvation, but even then it was baptism into the Church that was seen as making salvation available. Initiation into the Church means incorporation in the body of Christ and hence into his death and resurrection, symbolized in the ancient rite by actual immersion into and reemergence from the baptismal waters. This sacrament therefore symbolized the fact that what we as Christians call salvation comes initially and continually through participation in Christ's redemptive suffering and rebirth, and that this mystery is at the very heart of our reality as a church.

The sacrament which epitomizes the Church's liturgical life is the Eucharist. Through its association with Christ's death and resurrection it signifies the same redemptive mystery as baptism. Through its bringing Christians into experiential contact with that mystery it is a source of strength and healing. Through its call for conversion and reconciliation it is a sacrament of mutual forgiveness. Through its symbolic sharing of Christ's body and blood it is an expression and cause of unity within the Church. And through its call to self-sacrifice and its mediation of the divine power which makes self-sacrificing love possible, it is an exercise in both ministerial and communal priesthood. It is, in brief, the sacrament which summarizes the sacramentality of the

Church. Every time the Eucharist is celebrated it is saying, symbolically, that we are the body of Christ, participants in his redemptive mystery, a converted and loving community, a source of healing and forgiveness, an agent of reconciliation in the world, obedient and faithful to the Father, dedicated to the service of others. In reading and reflecting on God's word we proclaim that we are a listening and responding church; in the offering of gifts we announce that we are a self-sacrificing church; in the prayers of the canon we present ourselves as a dependent and thankful church; in the partaking of communion we symbolize that we are a sharing church.

Nevertheless, we can still ask, once the euphoria of such theological rhapsodizing has worn off: Is that what we are, really? Haven't we as a church often been the opposite of what our sacraments say we are? Can't we sometimes sense the hypocritical triumphalism that our critics accuse us of? Is it possible that more than occasionally our sacraments are false signs, symbolic lies, behind which we institutionally hide from the truth? And isn't the truth that we have often been, still are in many ways, and will undoubtedly persist in being a sinful, unforgiving and unredeemed assemblage of individuals?

Gregory Baum in *Religion and Alienation*, cited in Chapter II, argues that all too often the image of the Church as a social organization (that is, the organizational structure of the Church and the pattern of its institutional activities) does not correspond to the image of the Church found in its symbolic expressions (that is, in its liturgy and sacraments). And Juan Luis Segundo, whose *Sacraments Today* was discussed in Chapter IV, charges that this lack of correspondence is not merely incongruous but subversive: it undermines the sacraments and draws away their redemptive power.

And yet despite these criticisms from both outside and inside the Church, we continue to insist that the sacraments are important and even necessary. Not even Baum or Segundo, for example, suggest that as a church we should do away with them. Why is this? It is, I believe, because the unique spirit of Catholicism is found within the sacramental system itself. The sacraments make our church what it is. Despite all their shortcomings and despite all our failures, they make us a church, and they make us the particular incarnation of Christ that we are. They give us, in short, our Catholic identity.

For the sacraments are ecclesial symbols. They give us a common set of symbols with which we can identify as a church, over and above the scriptures and creeds with which all Christians can identify. They are the same seven sacraments for Catholics the world over, and they stretch back in time in one form or another across nearly twenty centuries of our institutional history. They have been the ritual vehicles for the continuous transmission of our common heritage. Even when we individually or collectively fail to live up to them, they signify what Catholicism claims to be and what we as Catholics believe we are.

They are, in this sense, prophetic symbols. Like the prophets of old they sometimes bring us the bad news that we are not what God wants us to be. By presenting us with images of what we ought to be as Christians and as a church, they pronounce God's judgment on the way we actually behave. But prophecy can also be the telling of good news, and the good news announced by the sacraments is that God makes it possible for us to be a faithful, reconciling, strengthening and serving community.

Thus the sacraments are also kerygmatic symbols. Not only do they announce in a general fashion the good news that salvation is possible, but they also apply that message to critical junctures in our individual and collective lives: birth, growth, unity, choice, estrangement, weakness, death. They give us in ritual and song, scripture and pastoral commentary, the word that we need to hear at that precise moment if we are to be what we claim to be, and what we sacramentally say we are.

For the sacraments are redemptive symbols. If we allow ourselves to listen to what God is telling us through them, if we open ourselves to the energizing grace that the Spirit communicates through them, they make salvation available and operative in the Church. When we consciously and deliberately enter into the mysteries which they present through symbolic representation, our minds and our hearts and our actions are transformed, sometimes in subtle and sometimes in dramatic ways.

Sacraments are therefore eschatological symbols. They bring about in sacred space and time a realization of the final times, when sin will be washed away, when divisions will be healed, when anger will be melted, when sorrow will be turned to joy, when death will have no sting. They give us hope for the future by making it present here and now.

But the sacraments do this because they are liturgical symbols. They are symbols which invite us into an attitude of prayer and worship, and through which we pass into that very same attitude. Moreover, we do this not singly but together, not as individuals but as a church. Which is why they form and transform not only our personal spirit but also our ecclesial spirit.

The sacraments are therefore the symbols that make us Catholic and that make us a church. Were we to eliminate them we might still be a church, for there are non-liturgical churches and there are other churches without all seven of the Catholic sacraments. But these are not catholic churches; they do not have our historical or global universality. Perhaps it would be more accurate to say, then, not that the sacraments make us a church, but that it is the sacraments that make us the Catholic Church, and that give Catholicism its particular spirit.

Furthermore, the sacraments are the symbols that make us individually Catholics. We can be Christians without these sacraments, for there are Christians who seem to do all right without them. Still, there seem to be few generic Christians in the world, that is, people who are neither Catholic nor Protestant nor Orthodox nor members of some other group that call themselves a Christian church, but who are still identifiably Christian. To become a Christian in any deep sense seems to necessitate that we identify with some Christian church and allow that church's spirit to shape our own.

Being a Catholic, therefore, means more than just being a Christian. It means being a Christian in a certain way, sharing in a certain ecclesial spirit. It means encountering the message of Jesus as it has been handed down through history within a definite community. And it means responding to God's grace in and through the symbolic rituals of that Church's tradition, the sacraments.

Recommended Reading

Karl Rahner, S.J., *Foundations of the Christian Faith* (New York: Seabury Press, 1978) Chapter 8.

Richard P. McBrien, *Catholicism* (Minneapolis: Winston Press, 1980) Chapters 21 and 22.

Louis Evely, *The Church and the Sacraments* (Denville, New Jersey: Dimension Books, 1971).

Peter Riga, *Sign and Symbol of the Invisible God* (Notre Dame, Indiana: Fides Publishers, 1971).

Ronald Sarno, S.J., *Let Us Proclaim the Mystery of Faith* (Denville, New Jersey: Dimension Books, 1970).

CHAPTER VIII: THE SACRAMENTS AND GLOBAL SPIRITUALITY

As Catholics we make much of our lengthy tradition and our world-wide presence: they are indicators of our catholicity. It is something to be proud of, but it also gives us a responsibility. For the Church is not in the world to be a monument to the past, it is there to be a leaven for the future. It is not there to be admired by people but to transform society.

Not very long ago the world was a very large place. Distant lands had unpronounceable names and foreign cities seemed strange and exotic. The people of those far away cultures were at least odd and sometimes even inscrutable.

It has become commonplace to say that the world has shrunk, but it is truer to say that we have stretched. Our eyes and ears reach around the planet through communications media. Our feet have been given wings by jet transportation. Our voice can travel anywhere through the telephone.

What has embraced the world in our lifetime is the Western technological spirit. And it has not only touched the far East and the southern hemisphere; it has transformed them. It has made them less strange. It has made them more like us. It has made them our neighbors.

Jesus was once asked, "Who is my neighbor?" In replying with the parable of the Good Samaritan, he said in essence that anyone you know about is your neighbor. But today we know about people who are affected by racism in our cities, poverty in our countryside, oppression in Latin America, suppression behind the Iron Curtain, starvation in Africa, antagonism in the Middle East, destitution in India: the list goes on.

Whether we like it or not, therefore, ours is a global spirit, for it encircles the world and it makes us conscious of people all over the planet. It is not necessarily our Christian or Catholic spirit, but it is mainly our Western, scientific and technological, political and economic spirit. Thus the question is posed, for those of us who call ourselves Catholics, should it also be a Christian spirit? That is to say, if the personal spirit of each of us has assumed global proportions, should it also be permeated by the spirit of God as revealed in the person of Jesus?

To give a flat No to that question would be schizophrenic, if we want to maintain that we are both Christian and modern. Like it or not, we are citizens of the world. Television and radio, newspapers and magazines have expanded our consciousness so that it now reaches around the planet. Yet our natural tendency is to withdraw into ourselves. We would prefer to think that we can live our personal lives and let the world go its own way. For Christians, this is also our perennial temptation. We would like to limit religion and make it a private affair, or at most a province of the Church. At one time in history, when our world and our awareness of it were both much smaller, that might have been possible, but the only way to do that today is to compartmentalize religion, to divorce it from what we know about so much of life. And that would be schizophrenic. At least for most of us.

But not for all of us. There are some whose world is inescapably small: the very young, the retarded, the illiterate, the impoverished. It is hard for them to see beyond their own needs, and so they really do not close their eyes to the needs of the global community. But this is not true of the rest of us. We see the slums in our cities, we read about the arms race, we hear about the unemployed, the underclothed, the underfed. And yet our spirit does not want to embrace them.

All too often our supposedly catholic spirit is in fact very provincial. Our Christian spirituality is a personal spirituality, a communal spirituality, and an ecclesial spirituality. And it stops there. But just as being a Christian individual implies membership in a Christian community, and just as being an individual parish implies participation in an ecclesial tradition, so also being Catholic has implications that reach beyond the Church and into the world at large.

Theologians today call the Church a sacrament. Indeed it is that. But that is also what it ought to be. A sacrament is a sign which mediates salvation; it is an instrument of grace. The Church then is and ought to be a medium of salvation. To some extent it is, but to some extent it is not and it ought to be. And to that extent it is not a sacrament. Likewise our parishes and other local gatherings are supposed to be sacramental communities. And in parallel fashion we too are each called to be sacramental persons. And yet so often we are not. Why?

Part of the answer lies in the nature of sacramental religion itself. The psychology of sacramental experience is that it takes us out of the secular world and into the realm of the sacred. It tends to be a private experience, and in its most intense moments it is intensely personal. The sociology of religious ritual shows that it tends to become ritualism. Often repeated ceremonies quickly become mechanical, forms of prayer and worship wither into empty formulas, and concern for their performance devolves into legalism. The history of religion during the classical phase in which Christianity began was characterized by a concern for salvation, for overcoming the estrangement between human beings and God. Yet despite theological nods in the direction of universal salvation, and despite occasional outbursts of missionary zeal, classical Christianity spoke mainly about individual redemption and about salvation within the Church. Not only did the Catholic sacraments reflect this mentality, but sacramental theology inevitably did so as well. The result is that even when theologians spoke about the social dimensions of the sacraments they hardly ever looked beyond the limits of the institutional Church.

Another part of the answer, however, lies in the fact that global consciousness is an entirely new phenomenon. Phenomenologically speaking, the world that most people lived in until the twentieth century was quite small: it reached only to the edges of their town, their region or, at most, their country. Maps in the Middle Ages, for example, did not cover much territory, and even at the beginning of modern times they still showed large tracts of unexplored areas. Even historical consciousness, the stretching of the imagination back in time and forward into the future, and the awareness that the past was really different from the present, is a relatively recent expansion of the human mind. Until the nineteenth century most people, including scientists, thought that the world was about six thousand years old, as it says in the Bible. So it would be anachronistic and somewhat unfair to expect earlier generations of Christians to have developed a global spirituality. Theirs was simply not a global spirit.

The challenge of developing such a spirituality is therefore ours. Fundamentally it is a task of allowing the dynamism of spiritual development to stretch beyond the confines of personal holiness and institutional sanctity, and to reshape first in our imagination and then in reality the world in which we live. The task is thus a dialectical one, for it is a matter of simultaneously acknowledging the Gospel message of salvation and confronting the global dimensions of a suffering humanity. Neither side of the dialectic can be denied, both must be affirmed, and each must be allowed to transform the other. For if there is a true dialogue between Christianity and the world (and theology in an incarnational church is committed to such a dialogue), ultimately neither one will remain the same.

Needless to say, the task of developing theology in a global spirit has already begun. Looking at it from a

Catholic viewpoint, we can say that it began with the social encyclicals of Leo XIII and Pius XI, the Knights of Labor and the Catholic Worker movement, and similar developments which attempted to apply Gospel principles to inequities in modern economic systems. In the middle of the present century, when biblical scholars were released from the burden of having to use scriptural quotations to prove Catholic dogmas, they were freed to find in the Bible social implications that had long been ignored. In the 1960s moral theology broke out of its long confinement to canon law and began to address questions of peace and justice in the light of the Gospel. In the 1970s liberation theologians in the Third World began to resist the restrictions of academic theologizing in order to translate Christianity into non-European terms. And in the 1980s fertile theological areas seem to be the Christian-Marxist dialogue and the attempt to find bonds of commonality among the world's great religions.

This bursting of the religious imagination beyond the boundaries of traditional teachings impels the sacramental theologian to reexamine the classical Christian rituals and to reevaluate them within a wider horizon. The issue is not one of negating what has been and still remains true on an individual, communal and ecclesial level, but of affirming that the meaning of the sacraments transcends all those levels of understanding.

The task, then, of sacramental theology on a global level is to work out the implications of the traditional Christian rituals for Catholics who are truly catholic in a contemporary sense. That is to say, the task is to initiate reflection on the central meaning of each of the sacraments and to ask: If we are to be faithful to that meaning, knowing what we do now about the world in which we live, how are we to live? Or to ask the same question in a different way: If our sacramental rituals are to be authentic signs of what we are — and we are, willingly or not, citizens of the world and members of a global community — what must we become? Or to put the question in dialectical terms: What are the discrepancies between our symbolic self-expressions and our actual selves, and how must each be changed if these discrepancies are to be overcome?

What then do the Catholic sacraments say we are? How do we fall short of that (bearing in mind that the New Testament word for sin, *hamartia*, means "to fall short") when we look at ourselves within a global perspective? And what do the sacraments themselves suggest that we must do or become in order to overcome this shortfall, that is, to authentically participate in the salvation of the world?

First of all, as already indicated, contemporary theology has expanded the meaning of the notion of sacramentality to include not only our ecclesiastical rituals but ourselves, our communities, and the Church itself. But calling ourselves sacraments is only pious rhetoric if nobody else knows it but us, and if we ourselves do not realize it until we hear it in a homily or read it in a book. Moreover, being a sacrament is not something that we should have to accept totally on faith; we should have some solid evidence for suspecting that it is true! That such concrete sacramentality is in fact a real possibility for us has been made evident by those individuals, groups and movements past and present, as well as by the Church as a whole, when they have been perceived by Christians and non-Christians alike as doing God's work, being signs of hope and instruments of salvation. And so the way to translate that possibility into actuality is also clear: simply do those things, individually, in groups and through ecclesiastical institutions, which alleviate human suffering, which overcome self-alienation and mutual estrangement, and which promote human self-transcendence and fulfillment. For sacraments participate in the realities that they signify. And so to bring such sacraments into existence, one need only to be instrumental in bringing such realities into existence.

Secondly, then, baptism is the sacrament of initiation into the Church, and it signifies immersion with Christ in death as well as rising with him transfigured. As we are reminded every Easter when we are asked to renew our baptismal promises, baptism is a sign that we have heard the Gospel, that we have renounced our allegiance to sin, and that we have accepted the way of Jesus as our own way of life. In the early days of Christianity, baptismal candidates were literally stripped naked, went down into and rose out of the baptismal pool, and were reclothed in white robes. It was a symbolic way of divesting oneself of the things of this world, of dissolving one's entanglement with sin, and of being reborn into a new life.

Viewed from a global perspective, baptism is arguably the sacrament of Gospel poverty, Christian renunciation and a transformed affirmation of life. In a world where three quarters of the people are poor, it can and should be a sign that we have renounced our attachment to whatever keeps them in poverty, and that we are engaged in activities which affirm our solidarity with their struggle for a fuller life. Individually baptism makes sense if I am continually contributing time and money to those who are in need, giving not out of my surplus but out of what I would need to maintain a standard of living which is grossly disproportional to theirs. In the local community baptism takes on a global dimension when it invites new members to live beneath their means and give to the poor, and when it makes it possible for them to do so in a way that is life affirming for both the giver and the receiver. And baptism is an honest sacrament of the universal Church when as an institution it relinquishes its attention to wealth and through its institutions it identifies itself with the poor, the hungry, the naked and the homeless. For baptism is above all a sign of having died to one way of life and of having been reborn into another.

Thirdly, confirmation as the completion of baptism is its complement. It signifies the fulness of life which comes from drawing one's vitality from the spirit of God, which is the spirit of Jesus, which is the Holy Spirit. It is the energy which can fill our hearts once we have emptied ourselves of our own self-concern. But in the sacramental ritual that spirit symbolically comes to us through the action of the bishop, who in turn is acting on behalf of the community.

Thus the new life that baptism symbolically promises and begins is an empowerment toward self-transcendence which comes not in isolation from others but from our openness to being strengthened by them. And conversely, as bearers of that life we communicate it to others through our concern and commitment to them, that is, through touching them.

As a sacrament of God's spirit in the world, therefore, confirmation is a sign of our faith in the communicability of that spirit to others. Ours is largely a world of despair, in which the impoverished have no hope of human betterment and in which the wealthy have no hope of escaping a nuclear holocaust. In either case there is no future, and where there is no future, there is no hope. Hope is possible only if there is energy available to change the present course of events. As an individual, therefore, I can affirm the symbolic truth of my confirmation if I am working to change the world's situation, thus reversing the downward spiral of despair in those to whom the energy for change is passed. As parishes we do the same when we make social concerns a part of our community commitment not only in words but also in deeds, beginning with the poor in our own neighborhood and reaching outward to the hungry of the world. And as a church Catholicism acts out what it symbolizes in confirmation when it commits its spiritual energies to social justice, nuclear disarmament, and world peace. For confirmation is, among other things, a sign that the power needed to change the world and redeem the future is available here and now.

Fourthly, penance is the sacrament of reconciliation in the Church, and it stands as a perpetual sign of our failure to fully live the Gospel. It therefore symbolizes our continuous need to overcome our estrangement from each other and from our deepest self, and in doing so to lessen our separation from God. More importantly, however, it signifies that such reconciliation is indeed possible if we would but accept it from God and work toward it with others. Nevertheless, since the Middle Ages penance has suffered from a privatization which suggested that forgiveness by God was all that was needed, and from a legalization which suggested that conformity to law was all that was asked. In early Christianity, however, when penance was called for it was a public enactment of repentance and forgiveness, and what was aimed at was not legalistic conformity but social reintegration.

Today, then, our more total awareness of alienation in the world makes penance a reminder that we are still too spiritually separated from our global neighbors, and that we in fact are a cause of much of their misery. The world's wealth is not well distributed, partly the result of our own overconsumption. The world is not at peace, partly the result of our own economic and ideological priorities. The world's poor suffer indignity and injustice, partly the result of our support for oppressive governments. The sacramental call for reconciliation therefore makes me aware of my personal guilt for the suffering of the world to which I would rather close my eyes, but at the same time it reminds me that international peace and cooperation are possible if I work towards them. Communal penance services are likewise sacraments of global reconciliation if on the one hand they awaken our sense of social sinfulness and on the other hand offer real possibilities for doing more than beating our breasts about them. And reconciliation at the ecclesial level reaches global dimensions when the Church is instrumental in mediating conflicts and reducing tensions between hostile groups in the world. All too often, it seems, the Church has been actively or passively a party to war, but this does not mean that it cannot or should not be a sacrament of peace; it means only that it has not heeded the global implications of its own ecclesiastical rite.

Fifthly, however, the Church's commitment to what is symbolized by the anointing of the sick is much more evident both in history and in the present. Hospitals began in the Middle Ages as extensions of the monastic rule of hospitality, even in patristic times clerics were caring for orphans and widows, and the New Testament itself mentions collections for the poor and other ministries to the needy. For the past ten centuries or so, the ecclesiastical rite which came to be called extreme unction was directed toward spiritual care for the dying rather than toward physical care for the sick, but even here the sacrament was a sign of God's concern for the helpless in their hour of need. As an anointing, this sacrament like confirmation is a symbolic strengthening, but its focus is on the strength that individuals need to cope with their debilities rather than on the strength needed to go forth and help others.

Viewed in terms of the world's suffering, the anointing of the sick points to those millions who will never be rescued from sickness and starvation in time to escape their premature death. Our natural inclination is to forget about them and let them die, but Christ's words and the Church's tradition tell us that even the least are worthy of our attention. I personally live the meaning of this sacrament, therefore, when I keep the helpless in my heart, resisting the temptation to dismiss them as deserving of their lot, arguing with myself and others that we owe them care and aid for no other reason than that they are suffering. Likewise, our parish celebrations of anointing take on global significance when they are done in a community which, besides extending itself to comfort its own members, is working to touch the physically and emotionally wounded of the world beyond its parish boundaries. And the Church too is a sacrament of global healing and caring insofar as it continues to be an institution through which people can help the helpless not in the name of progress but simply in the name of love.

Sixthly, marriage is the sacrament of fidelity and devotion between Christian men and women living in a lasting relationship. The Christian tradition since the days of St. Paul has taken as the model of that relationship the commitment of Christ to the Church and of the Church to its Lord. Thus Christian marriage has always been understood to be a relationship of love "in the Lord," not based on mutual attraction or the benefits to be gotten out of it, but based on mutual self-giving and the good that it bears for one's spouse, children and even the family that extends beyond that nucleus. In fact, the nuclear family as we know it today is a fairly recent invention of Western society, a product of the industrial revolution. In agricultural societies still, the extended family of in-laws and cousins and other relatives is the basic social group to which people owe their love and in which they find their home.

The Church sometimes calls itself the family of God, and both here and in the local community the human paradigm for it is not the nuclear family but the extended family. Marriage as a Catholic sacrament therefore is not only a sign of fidelity between spouses but also a symbol of their acceptance of the larger family into which they are entering. As such it is a sign of their willingness to orient themselves to the well being of others not as a part-time service but as a full-time commitment. Viewed in its widest context, therefore, the sacrament of marriage implies not only a willingness to establish a lasting relationship with a new natural family, but it also suggests a concern for the whole human family as well. It means that I broaden my perception of the family to which I belong and look upon all people as my own brothers and sisters, parents and children. In the parish it means that we take an active interest in the well being of families, the education of children, the social needs of the aged, the unemployed, the imprisoned, the handicapped, and so on. And in the institutional Church it means working for social and economic structures that promote the good of natural families and family-style communities, and sponsoring organized efforts not only to foster family life but also to help people deal with the stresses and breakdowns which, in the larger picture, are inevitable in close human relationships.

Seventhly, holy orders is the sacrament of Christian ministry, and although for a good deal of the Church's history ministry was identified with clerical priesthood, a broader study of history and a fuller appreciation for ministry in the Church today reveals that what is involved here is more than sacramental administration and other clerical functions. As an ecclesiastical ritual, ordination is a sign through which a person accepts the call of the community to lead it in prayer and worship and other aspects of church-related life. But it is also a sign through which the Church as a religious society affirms that there are certain tasks that must be performed, and to which individuals must be appointed, if it is to be a church at all.

If one conceives of the Church narrowly so that the word is the equivalent of "clergy" or "hierarchy," then ministry in the Church is necessarily limited to the formally ordained priesthood. But if one conceives of the Church broadly so as to include all its members, clergy and laity alike, then both the notion of ministry and opportunities for it are likewise broadened. Within this wider perspective only a fraction of the Church's ministers are ordained, for there are many who minister to the needs of the Church without ever being commissioned to do so in an ecclesiastical ceremony: teachers, administrators, pastoral workers, musicians, liturgical assistants, and so on. The official sacrament of orders is therefore symbolic of ministry, but it is not in any way coextensive with it.

Now, ministry in either the narrow or the broad sense is ordinarily conceived of as service within the Church. But what then is the ministry or service of the Church itself? Its mission and therefore its service is to the world, and so the notion of ministry as applied to the whole Church necessarily has a global dimension to it. As an individual Catholic, therefore, I participate in the Church's ministry to the world when I respond to the needs of those outside the Church. Parishes do the same when they sponsor local efforts and support more distant attempts to meet the human needs of non-Catholics, and when they encourage their members to pursue lives of service to others rather than careers of profit to themselves. The Church as an organization is inescapably involved with ministry, to be sure, but that ministry takes on a global dimension when it is directed outward, to meeting the spiritual and physical needs of persons and groups not in the Church, or to addressing problems in the secular society in which it finds itself.

Eighth and finally there is Eucharist, which is the sacramental celebration of who we are as followers of Jesus, as a Christian community and as the Church. It is, as its name implies, a celebration of thanksgiving for all that we are and all that we have received from God through Christ and through each other. It is a listening and responding to God's word, not singly but together. It is an offering in which, with Christ, we give ourselves back to our Father in return for all that he has given us. It is a meal in which bread and wine are blessed and shared, in commemoration of Christ's death and resurrection, and as a sign of what we ourselves are called to do.

In our Eucharistic worship, therefore, in union with those present, we unite ourselves with the whole Church and by extension with all of humanity in an act of self-giving thanks. In accepting the bread that is broken and the cup that is shared, we identify ourselves with our Lord whose body was beaten and whose blood was shed so that others might live. Such an act permeates my global consciousness and affirms my commitment to the world, therefore, to the extent that I am already thankful not only for what I myself have received but for all the good things of both natural and human creation, and to the extent that I am already aware that so much is still not enough when so many have so little. The Eucharist is also a fitting sign of our communal dependence on God and of our self-giving to the world in the measure that together we acknowledge our dependence on other people and together we commit ourselves to sharing the world's abundance with them. And the Eucharist is an act of global worship in the Church to the extent that as a world-wide organization it pours itself out in sacrifice for the salvation of all people.

The global implications of the sacraments, therefore, tell us that today we must be in the world at large what we have always acknowledged we must be as Christians: those who are willing to surrender themselves to Christ and the Gospel, those who would give rather than receive, those who love their enemies and bless those who hate them, those who are prepared to commit their lives to the world's redemption, those who by their words and actions are announcing the arrival of the kingdom of God. For if it is a truly dialectical relationship between ourselves as Christians and the world in which we live, a dialogue that is mediated through the Church's sacramental worship, then as indicated earlier in this chapter, neither we nor the world will remain the same.

But there is also another dimension to the dialectic that was suggested, namely that through such a dialogue the sacraments themselves would be changed. What we have now in the Catholic Church is a system of seven sacramental rituals that have evolved through twenty centuries of history. But that history has run its course mainly within the confines of European Christianity. The liturgical forms of the Catholic Church are therefore at the present time not only Christian but also predominately European, even though some of them have Middle Eastern origins and elements. As if underscoring this fact, the recent revisions of the sacraments endorsed by the Second Vatican Council and promulgated by Rome were by and large reworkings of the traditional European rites, and the revisions themselves were made by liturgists trained in the Western theological tradition.

At the present time, however, Catholicism as a world religion is breaking out of the European mold in which it was formed, and it is pouring itself into the cultures of Latin America, Africa and Asia. True, it had sent missionaries there in the past, but the colonial Catholicism that they brought with them was Roman in both name and style, whereas today both missionaries and native clergy see the importance of allowing cultural diversity into the Church. Is it not reasonable to expect, then, that in the course of time the Church in those regions will develop sacramental forms which are quite different from ours today? After all, the Church's present sacraments developed in dialogue with European culture over the course of centuries, sometimes through a series of startlingly different mutations. How many early Christians, for instance, would have recognized the grandiose patristic liturgies as the descendants of the

Lord's Supper which they shared around a table in their homes? Or for that matter, how many patristic bishops would have acknowledged that the private Mass of the Middle Ages, offered silently by a single priest with no congregation, could be the lineal offspring of episcopal liturgies concelebrated with many ministers, attended by throngs of the faithful, and embellished with hymns and responses? The words of the sacraments, the sacramental gestures themselves, and even the material elements in them have all changed to a greater or lesser extent through the ages.

Today we look back at the first century or two of Christianity as the "early days" of the Church. But what if the world is still around two hundred centuries from now? Isn't it conceivable that historians then will call us the "early" Christians? From such a futural as well as global perspective, therefore, it seems futile to restrict the coming course of sacramental history to a narrow continuation of its past history. Especially if Christianity continues its dialogue with the world — this time a world of many cultures — we can expect both a transformation of the world and a transformation of the Church.

That transformation of the Church, however, will in fact make it more catholic. Until now our catholicity has been spatial and temporal, but it has also been monocultural. Now, the ongoing globalization of the Church will make it more polycultural or, if you will, pluralistic. Of course, there is as was stated earlier a growing secular and technical mentality which is enveloping our planet, and this is having its own impact on the cultures that it touches. But in its dialectical transformation of the cultures of different regions, it itself is transformed in various ways, so that cultural differences remain. And a Catholic spirituality, even a Catholic sacramental spirituality, must come to terms both with the technological spirit of the age and with the cultural spirits of various peoples around the globe. The resulting Catholicism may not be as homogeneous as it has been in the past (actually, in the recent past, for during the first thousand years of Christian history there was much more cultural diversity among the churches of the Middle East, North Africa, and Europe), but it will be more universal. And it may be harder to define the Catholic spirit and to describe the Catholic sacraments when this happens, except in a way which allows for a pluralistic spirituality and which tolerates a plurality of sacramental forms.

But we should not anticipate the coming sacramental revolution with dread, nor with premature nostalgia for the good old days of Vatican II. It is the business of sacramental worship to transform us inwardly and outwardly, by awakening in us the dynamics of religious self-transcendence, and by making available the grace to be what we are called by God to be. And it is the heritage of a sacramental church to develop those liturgical rites which mediate the eternal in a symbolic language which is always contemporary.

Recommended Reading

Rafael Avila, *Worship and Politics* (Maryknoll, New York: Orbis Books, 1981).

Monika K. Hellwig, *The Eucharist and the Hunger of the World* (New York: Paulist Press, 1976).

Tissa Balasuria, O.M.I., *The Eucharist and Human Liberation* (Maryknoll, New York: Orbis Books, 1979).

Vincent J. Donovan, C.S.Sp., *Christianity Rediscovered: An Epistle from the Masai* (Notre Dame: Fides/Claretian, 1978).

Robert Muller, *New Genesis: Shaping a Global Spirituality* (New York: Doubleday, 1982).

CONCLUSION

The sacraments are not an end in themselves; they are a means to an end. More precisely, they are means to many ends on four distinct levels of spiritual development.

On the individual level, they bring us to an awareness of who we are as Christians, called by God to self-transcendence and personal conversion. Baptism and confirmation, for example, invite us to stop living for ourselves and to start living for others, to die with Christ in the waters which dissolve our self-centeredness and to be reborn with a new spirit of self-giving. Penance draws us into a process of self-examination, reconversion and recommitment to a career of continuous dedication to the ideals of the Gospel. The Eucharist tells us to sacrifice our egoistic concerns and to become concerned with offering ourselves to God in union with Christ. And by consciously entering into what the sacraments symbolize, we allow them to transform our consciousness and our behavior so that we become the reality that they signify. We make it real. We incarnate it in our very being. And in doing so, we ourselves become sacraments signifying what God has done in us and what surrender to the spirit of Christ can do for others.

On the social level, the sacraments are means to the end of community building and social transformation. They make us aware of the interpersonal dimensions of our conversion and of our commitment to the task of self-transcendence. Christian intiation, for example, is nothing if it is not the beginning of a life shared with others. Christian marriage is not Christian at all if it is not a life of dedication to the well being of one's spouse and children. Christian worship is not truly liturgy if it does not give us a sense of our union with and commitment to those with whom we pray. On the other hand, by deliberately dedicating ourselves to what the sacraments symbolize, we open ourselves to a new dimension of interpersonal relationships, and we begin to participate in the reality that they signify. Christian community comes into being where it was not before, and it is intensified where it already existed. And when this happens, Christian families, friendships, parishes, schools and other organized groups become sacraments themselves, signifying the transforming power of grace in human relationships and symbolizing the direction that the transformation of the human community should take.

On the ecclesial level, the sacraments make us aware of our heritage as Christians and our identity as Catholics. The sacrament of anointing, for example, reminds us that care for the sick and the dying is a perennial Christian concern and so we cannot be insensitive to those who are suffering nor blind to those who are dying if we call ourselves followers of Jesus. The sacrament of orders likewise tells us that the Church in history is not the result of charismatic serendipity and so it needs organization in its ministry. The sacrament of the Eucharist, in the same way, as the central and traditional act of Christian worship, identifies our own liturgy with the public prayer of Christians across twenty centuries and unites us with all ecclesial communities around the world that call themselves Catholic. By intentionally embracing such sacramental forms of worship as our own, we become members of the transhistorical and transcultural reality that they signify. We make it real in present history and in our present situation. And in doing so the Church itself becomes an identifiable sign of Christ's presence in the world, a unified sacrament of the Christian message and divine grace.

Lastly, on the global level, the sacraments are a means to the transformation of the world and the salvation of the larger human community. At this level their effects (even their potential effects) are not as direct or immediate as those which they have (or can have) on the first three levels. Nevertheless, insofar as sacramental worship does effect a transformation of individual consciousness and personal behavior, insofar as it calls the Church into being and energizes it as a medium of divine life in human history, to that extent sacramental worship plays a real role in the redemption of the world.

As Catholics today we must admit that the understanding of the sacraments which we inherited from medieval scholasticism and Tridentine dogmatism was rather limited. The effectiveness of the sacraments is not as neat nor as automatic as it once seemed to be. Their institution by Christ is not as directly traceable to Jesus of Nazareth as it once appeared to be. Even their numbering as seven is not as absolute and eternal as we once assumed it was. Nevertheless, that traditional understanding of the sacraments was about as broad and sophisticated as Christians could make it, given the limitations of human knowlege and social experience within which it developed.

In our own day, however, psychology and sociology have given us new instruments of analysis, our knowledge of history has become more detailed and nuanced, and new varieties of philosophy and theology have increased the number of perspectives from which we may view sacramental worship. Within such an expanded horizon we can see that the seven traditional sacraments are still valid and fruitful, but the meaning of their validity and fruitfulness has been transformed. Their validity today is rooted in their ability to express what is actually going on in the experience of individuals, local communities, the Church as a whole, and humanity as such. And their fruitfulness is measured by the transforming effects that they have on persons, groups, the Church at large, and the history of the human endeavor itself.